Arthur W. Pink Collection Vol 1

Arthur W. Pink Collection Vol 1

The Divine Inspiration of the Bible
Profiting From The Word
Divine Healing: Is It Scriptural

Arthur W. Pink

©2011 Bottom of the Hill Publishing
All rights reserved. No part of this book may be used or reproduced in any manner without written permission except for brief quotations for review purposes only.

Printed in the United States of America and Australia.

Bottom of the Hill Publishing
Memphis, TN
www.BottomoftheHillPublishing.com

ISBN: 978-1-61203-544-4

Contents

The Divine Inspiration of the Bible   6

Profiting From The Word   85

Divine Healing: Is It Scriptural?   167

Arthur W. Pink

The Divine Inspiration of the Bible

Content

CHAPTER ONE	12
CHAPTER TWO	16
CHAPTER THREE	19
CHAPTER FOUR	26
CHAPTER FIVE	35
CHAPTER SIX	41
CHAPTER SEVEN	53
CHAPTER EIGHT	57
CHAPTER NINE	60
CHAPTER TEN	64
CHAPTER ELEVEN	67
CHAPTER TWELVE	71
CHAPTER THIRTEEN	75
CHAPTER FOURTEEN	81

Arthur W. Pink

INTRODUCTION

Christianity is the religion of a Book. Christianity is based upon the impregnable rock of Holy Scripture. The starting point of all doctrinal discussion must be the Bible. Upon the foundation of the Divine inspiration of the Bible stands or falls the entire edifice of Christian truth.—"If the foundations be destroyed, what can the righteous do?" (Ps. 11:3). Surrender the dogma of verbal inspiration and you are left like a rudderless ship on a stormy sea-at the mercy of every wind that blows. Deny that the Bible is, without any qualifications, the very Word of God, and you are left without any ultimate standard of measurement and without any supreme authority. It is useless to discuss any doctrine taught by the Bible until you are prepared to acknowledge, unreservedly, that the Bible is the final court of appeal. Grant that the Bible is a Divine revelation and communication of God's own mind and will to men, and you have a fixed starting point from which advance can be made into the domain of truth. Grant that the Bible is (in its original manuscripts) inerrant and infallible and you reach the place where study of its contents is both practicable and profitable.

It is impossible to over-estimate the importance of the doctrine of the Divine inspiration of Scripture. This is the strategic center of Christian theology, and must be defended at all costs. It is the point at which our satanic enemy is constantly hurling his hellish battalions. Here it was he made his first attack. In Eden he asked, "Yea, hath God said?" and today he is pursuing the same tactics. Throughout the ages the Bible has been the central object of his assaults. Every available weapon in the devil's arsenal has been employed in his determined and ceaseless efforts to destroy the temple of God's truth. In the first days of the Christian era the attack of the enemy was made openly—the bonfire being the chief instrument of destruction—but, in these "last days" the assault is made in a more subtle manner and comes from a more unexpected quarter. The Divine origin of the Scriptures is now disputed in the name of "Scholarship" and "Science," and that, too, by those who profess to be friends and champions of the Bible. Much of

The Divine Inspiration of the Bible

the learning and theological activity of the hour, are concentrated in the attempt to discredit and destroy the authenticity and authority of God's Word, the result being that thousands of nominal Christians are plunged into a sea of doubt. Many of those who are paid to stand in our pulpits and defend the Truth of God are now the very ones who are engaged in sowing the seeds of unbelief and destroying the faith of those to whom they minister. But these modern methods will prove no more successful in their efforts to destroy the Bible than did those employed in the opening centuries of the Christian era. As well might the birds attempt to demolish the granite rock of Gibraltar by pecking at it with their beaks—"Forever, O Lord, Thy Word is settled in heaven" (Ps. 119:89).

Now the Bible does not fear investigation. Instead of fearing it, the Bible courts and challenges consideration and examination. The more widely it is known, the more closely it is read, the more carefully it is studied, the more unreservedly will it be received as the Word of God. Christians are not a company of enthusiastic fanatics. They are not lovers of myths. They are not anxious to believe a delusion. They do not desire their lives to be molded by an empty superstition. They do not wish to mistake hallucination for inspiration. If they are wrong, they wish to be set right. If they are deceived, they want to be disillusioned. If they are mistaken, they desire to be corrected.

The first question which the thoughtful reader of the Bible has to answer is, What importance and value am I to attach to the contents of the Scriptures? Were the writers of the Bible so many fanatics moved by oracular frenzy? Were they merely poetically inspired and intellectually elevated? or, were they, as they claimed to be, and as the Scriptures affirm they were, moved by the Holy Spirit to act as the voice of God to a sinful world? Were the writers of the Bible inspired by God in a manner no other men were in any other age of the world? Were they invested and endowed with the power to disclose mysteries and point men upward and onward to that which otherwise would have been an impenetrable future? One can readily appreciate the fact that the answer to these questions is of supreme importance. If the Bible is not inspired in the strictest sense of the word then it is worthless, for it claims to be God's Word, and if its claims are spurious then its statements are unreliable and its contents are untrustworthy. If, on the other hand, it can be shown to the satisfaction of every impartial inquirer that the Bible is the Word of God, inerrant and infallible, then we have a starting point from which we can advance to the conquest of all truth.

A book that claims to be a Divine revelation—a claim which, as we shall see, is substantiated by the most convincing credentials—cannot be rejected or even neglected without grave peril to the soul. True wisdom cannot refuse to examine it with care and impartiality. If the claims of the Bible be well founded then the prayerful and diligent study of the Scriptures becomes of paramount importance: they have a claim upon our notice and time which nothing else has, and beside them everything in this world loses its luster and sinks into utter insignificance. If the Bible be the Word of God then it infinitely transcends in value all the writings of men, and in exact ratio to its immeasurable superiority to human productions such is our responsibility and duty to give it the most reverent and serious consideration. As a Divine revelation the Bible ought to be studied, yet, this is the only subject on which human curiosity does not desire information. Into every other sphere man pushes his investigations, but the Book of books is neglected, and this, not only by the ignorant, and illiterate, but by the wise of this world as well. The cultured dilettante will boast of his acquaintance with the sages of Greece and Rome, yet, will know little or nothing of Moses and the prophets, Christ and His Apostles. But the general neglect of the Bible verifies the Scriptures and affords additional proof of their authenticity. The contempt with which the Bible is treated demonstrates that human nature is exactly what God's Word represents it to be—fallen and depraved—and is unmistakable evidence that the carnal mind is enmity against God.

If the Bible is the Word of God; if it stands on an infinitely exalted plane, all alone; if it immeasurable transcends all the greatest productions of human genius; then, we should naturally expect to find that it has unique credentials, that there are internal marks which prove it to be the handiwork of God, that there is conclusive evidence to show that its Author is superhuman, Divine. That these expectations are realized we shall now endeavor to show; that there is no reason whatever for anyone to doubt the Divine inspiration of the Scriptures is the purpose of this book to demonstrate. As we examine the natural world we find innumerable proofs of the existence of a Personal Creator, and the same God

The Divine Inspiration of the Bible

who has manifested Himself through His works has also revealed His wisdom and will through His Word. The God of creation and the God of written revelation are One, and there are irrefutable arguments to show that the Almighty who made the heavens and the earth is also the Author of the Bible.

We shall now submit to the critical attention of the reader a few of the lines of demonstration which argue for the Divine inspiration of the Bible.

Arthur W. Pink

CHAPTER ONE
THERE IS A PRESUMPTION IN FAVOR OF THE BIBLE

This argument may be simply and tersely stated thus—Man needed a Divine revelation couched in human language. God had previously given man a revelation of Himself in His created works—which men please to term "nature" —but bears unmistakable testimony to the existence of its Creator, and though sufficient is revealed of God through it to render all men "without excuse," yet creation does not present a complete unveiling of God's character. Creation reveals God's wisdom and power, but it gives us a very imperfect presentation of His mercy and love. Creation is now under the curse; it is imperfect, because it has been marred by sin; therefore, an imperfect creation cannot be a perfect medium for revealing God; and hence, also, the testimony of creation is contradictory.

In the spring of the year, when nature puts on her loveliest robes and we see the beautiful foliage of the countryside and listen to the happy songs of the birds, we have no difficulty in inferring that a gracious God is ruling over our world. But what of the winter-time, when the countryside is desolate and the trees are leafless and forlorn, when a pall of death seems to be resting on everything? When we stood by the seashore and watched the setting sun crimsoning the placid waters on a quiet eve, we had no hesitation in ascribing the picture to the hand of the Divine Artist. But when we stand upon the same seashore on a stormy night, hear the roaring of the breakers and the howling wind, see the boats battling with the angry waves and listen to the heart-rending cries of the seamen as they go down into a watery grave, then, we are tempted to wonder if, after all, a merciful God is at the helm. As one walks through the Grand Canyon or stands before the Niagara Falls, the hand and power of God seem very evident; but, as one witnesses the desolations of the San Francisco earthquake or the

The Divine Inspiration of the Bible

death-dealing effects of the volcanic eruptions of Mount Vesuvius, he is again perplexed and puzzled. In a word then, the testimony of nature is conflicting, and, as we have said, this is due to the fact that sin has come in and marred God's handiwork. Creation displays God's natural attributes but it tells us little or nothing of His moral perfections. Nature knows no forgiveness and shows no mercy, and if we had no other source of information we should never discover the fact that God pardons sinners. Man then needs a written revelation from God.

Our limitations and our ignorance reveal our need. Man is in darkness concerning God. Blot the Bible out of existence and what should we know about His character, His moral attributes, His attitude toward us, or His demands upon us? As we have seen, nature is but an imperfect medium for revealing God. The ancients had the same nature before them as we have, but what did they discover of His character? Unto what knowledge of the one true God did they attain? The seventeenth chapter of the Acts answers that question. When the Apostle Paul was in the famous city of Athens, famous for its learning and philosophical culture, he discovered an altar, on which were inscribed the words, "To the unknown God". The same condition prevails today. Visit those lands which have not been illumined by the light of the Holy Scriptures and it will be found that their peoples know no more about the character of the living God than did the ancient Egyptians and Babylonians.

Man is in darkness concerning himself. From whence am I? What am I? Am I anything more than a reasoning animal? Have I an immortal soul, or, am I nothing more than a sentient being? What is the purpose of my existence? Why am I here in this world at all? What is the end and aim of life? How shall I employ my time and talents? Shall I live only for today, eat, drink, and be merry? What after death? Do I perish like the beasts of the field, or is the grave the portal into another world? If so, whither am I bound? Do these questions appear senseless and irrelevant? Annihilate the Scriptures, eliminate all the light they have shed upon these problems, and whither shall we turn for a solution? If the Bible had never been written how many of these questions could have been satisfactorily answered? A very striking testimony to man's need of a Divine revelation was given by the celebrated but skeptical historian Gibbon. He remarked—"Since, therefore, the most sublime efforts of philosophy can extend no farther than feebly to point out the desire, the hope, or, at most, the probability, of a future state, there is nothing except a Divine revelation that can ascertain the existence and describe the condition of the invisible country which is destine to receive the souls of men after their separation from the body."

Our experiences reveal our need. There are problems to be faced which our wisdom is incapable of solving; there are obstacles in our path which we have no means of surmounting; there are enemies to be met which we are unable to vanquish. We are in dire need of counsel, strength, and courage. There are trials and tribulations which come to us, testing the hearts of the bravest and stoutest, and we need comfort and cheer. There are sorrows and bereavements which crush our spirits and we need the hope of immortality and resurrection.

Our corporate life reveals our need. What is to govern and regulate our dealings one with the other? Shall each do that which is right in his own eyes? That would destroy all law and order. Shall we draw up some moral code, some ethical standard? But who shall fix it? Opinions vary. We need some final court of appeal: if we had no Bible, where should we find it?

Man then needs a Divine revelation; God is able to supply that need; therefore, is it not reasonable to suppose He will do so? Surely God will not mock our ignorance and leave us to grope in the dark! If it is harder to believe that the universe had no creator, than it is to believe that "in the beginning God created the heavens and the earth;" if it is a greater tax upon our faith to suppose that Christianity with all its glorious triumphs is without a Divine Founder, than it is to believe that it rests upon the Person of the Lord Jesus Christ; then, does it not also make a greater demand upon human credulity to imagine that God would leave mankind without an intelligible communication from Himself, than it does to believe that the Bible is a revelation from the Creator to His fallen and erring creatures?

If there is a personal God (and none but a "fool" will deny His existence), and if we are the works of His hands He surely would not leave us in doubt concerning the great problems which have to do with our temporal, spiritual, and eternal welfare. If an earthly parent advises his sons and daughters in their problems and perplexities, warns them of the perils and pitfalls of life which menace their well-being; counsels them with regard to their daily welfare and makes known to them his plans and purposes concerning their future, surely it is incredible to suppose that our Heavenly Father would do less for His children!

We are often uncertain as to which is the right course to pursue; we are frequently in doubt as to the real path of duty; we are constantly surrounded by the hosts of wickedness which seek to accomplish our downfall; and, we are daily confronted with experiences which make us sad and sorrowful. The wisest among us need guidance which our own wisdom fails to supply; the best of humanity need grace which the human heart is powerless to bestow; the most refined among the sons of men need deliverance from temptations which they cannot overcome. Will God mock us then in our need? Will God leave us alone in the hour of our weakness? Will God refuse to provide for us a Refuge from our enemies? Man needs a Counselor, a Comforter, a Deliverer. The very fact that God has a Father's regard for His children necessitates that He should give them a written revelation which communicates His mind and will concerning them and which points them to the One who is willing and able to supply all their need.

To sum up this argument. Man needs a Divine revelation; God is able to supply one; is it not, therefore, reasonable to suppose He will do so? There is then, a presumption in favor of the Bible. Is it not more reasonable to believe that He whose name and nature is Love shall provide us with a lamp unto our feet and a light unto our path, than to leave us to grope our way amid the darkness of a fallen and ruined world?

Arthur W. Pink

CHAPTER TWO
THE PERENNIAL FRESHNESS OF THE BIBLE BEARS WITNESS TO ITS DIVINE INSPIRER

The full force of the present argument will appeal only to those who are intimately acquainted with the Bible, and the more familiar the reader is with the Sacred Canon the more heartily will he endorse the following statements. Just as a knowledge of Latin is necessary in order to understand the technique of a treatise on pathology or physiology, or just as a certain amount of culture and academic learning is an indispensable adjunct to intelligently follow the arguments and apprehend the illustrations in a dissertation on philosophy or psychology, so a first-hand acquaintance with the Bible is necessary to appreciate the fact that its contents never become commonplace.

One of the first facts which arrests the attention of the student of God's Word is that, like the widow's oil and meal which nourished Elijah, the contents of the Bible are never exhausted. Unlike all other books, the Bible never acquires a sameness, and never diminishes in its power of response to the needy soul which comes to it. Just as a fresh supply of manna was given each day to the Israelites in the wilderness, so the Spirit of God ever breaks anew the Bread of Life to them who hunger after righteousness; or, just as the loaves and fishes in the hands of our Lord were more than enough to feed the famished multitude—a surplus still remaining—so the honey and milk of the Word are more than sufficient to satisfy the hunger of every human soul—the supply still remaining undiminished for new generations.

Although one may know, word for word, the entire contents of some chapter of Scripture, and although he may have taken the time to ponder thoughtfully every sentence therein, yet, on every subsequent occasion, provided one comes to it again in the spirit

The Divine Inspiration of the Bible

of humble inquiry, each fresh reading will reveal new gems never seen there before and new delights will be experienced never met with previously. The most familiar passages will yield as much refreshment at the thousandth perusal as they did at the first. The Bible has been likened to a fountain of living water: the fountain is ever the same, but the water is always fresh.

Herein the Bible differs from all other books, sacred or secular. What man has to say can be gathered from his writings at the first reading: failure to do so indicates that the writer has not succeeded in expressing himself clearly, or else the reader has failed to apprehend his meaning. Man is only able to deal with surface things, hence he cares only about surface appearances; consequently, whatever man has to say lies upon the surface of his writings, and the capable reader can exhaust them by a single perusal. Not so with the Bible. Although the Bible has been studied more microscopically than any other book (even its very letters have been counted and registered) by many of the keenest intellects for the past two thousand years, although whole libraries of works have been written as commentaries upon its teachings, and although literally millions of sermons have been preached and printed in the attempt to expound every part of Holy Writ, yet its contents have not been exhausted, and in this twentieth century new discoveries are being made in it every day!

The Bible is an inexhaustible mine of wealth: it is the El Dorado of heavenly treasure. It has veins of ore which never "give out" and pockets of gold which no pick can empty; yet, like earthly treasures, the gems of God must be diligently sought if they are to be found. Potatoes lie near the surface of the ground, but diamonds require much laborious digging, so also the precious things of the Word are only revealed to the prayerful, patient and diligent student.

The Bible is like a spring of water which never runs dry. No matter how many may drink from its life-giving stream, and no matter how often they may quench their thirst at its refreshing waters, its flow continues and never fails to satisfy the needs of all who come and take of its perennial springs. The Bible has a whole continent of Truth yet to be explored. A learned scholar who died during the present year of grace had read through the Bible no fewer than five hundred times! What other book, ancient or modern, Oriental or Occidental, would repay even a fiftieth reading?

How can we account for this marvelous characteristic of the Bible? What explanation can we offer for this startling phenomenon? It is only stating a commonplace axiom when we affirm that what is finite is fathomable. What the mind of man has produced the mind of man can exhaust. If human mortals had written the Bible its contents would have been "mastered" ages ago. In view of the fact that the contents of the Scriptures cannot be exhausted, that they never acquire sameness or staleness to the devout student, and that they always speak with fresh force to the quickened soul that comes to them, is it not apparent that none other than the infinite mind of God could have created such a wonderful Book as the Bible?

CHAPTER THREE
THE UNMISTAKABLE HONESTY OF THE WRITERS OF THE BIBLE ATTESTS TO ITS HEAVENLY ORIGIN

The title of this chapter suggests a wide field of study the limits of which we can now only skirt here and there. To begin with the writers of the Old Testament.

Had the historical parts of the Old Testament been a forgery, or the production of uninspired men, their contents would have been very different to what they are. Each of its Books was written by a descendant of Abraham, yet nowhere do we find the bravery of the Israelites extolled and never once are their victories regarded as the outcome of their courage or military genius; on the contrary, success is attributed to the presence of Jehovah the God of Israel. To this it might be replied, Heathen writers have often ascribed the victories of their peoples to the intervention of their gods. This is true, yet there is no parallel at all between the two cases. Comparison is impossible. Heathen writers invariably represent their gods as being blindly partial to their friends and whenever their favorites failed to come out victorious their defeat is attributed to the opposition of other gods or to a blind and unyielding fate. In contradistinction to this, the defeats of Israel, as much as their victories, are regarded as coming from Jehovah. Their successes were not due to mere partiality in God, but are uniformly viewed as connected with a careful observance of His commands; and, in like manner, their defeats are portrayed as the outcome of their disobedience and waywardness. If they transgressed His laws they were defeated and put to shame, even though their God was the Almighty. But we have digressed somewhat. That to which we desire to direct attention is the fact that men who were their own countrymen have chronicled the history of the Israelites, and therein have faithfully recorded their defeats not to an inexorable fate, nor to bad generalship and military failures, but to the sins of the people and their wickedness against God. Such a God is not the creation of the human mind, and such historians were not actuated by the common principles of human nature.

Not only have the Jewish historians recounted the military defeats of their people, but they have also faithfully recorded their many moral backslidings and spiritual declinations. One of the outstanding truths of the Old Testament is that the Unity of God, that God is One, that beside Him there is none else, that all other gods are false gods and that to pay them homage is to be guilty of the sin of idolatry. Against the sin of idolatry these Jewish writers cry out repeatedly. They uniformly declare that it is a sin most abhorrent in the sight of heaven. Yet, these same Jewish writers record how again and again their ancestors (contrary to the universal leaning towards ancestral adoration and worship), and their contemporaries, were guilty of this great wickedness. Not only so, but they have pointed out how some of their most famous heroes sinned in this very particular. Aaron and the golden calf, Solomon and the later kings being notable examples—"Then did Solomon build a high place for Chemosh, the abomination of Moab, in the hill that is before Jerusalem, and for Molech, the abomination of the children of Ammon. And likewise did he for all his strange wives, which burnt incense and sacrificed unto their gods" (Kings 11:7,8). Moreover, there is no attempt made to excuse their wrongdoing; instead, their acts are openly censured and uncompromisingly condemned. As is well known, human historians are inclined to conceal or extenuate the faults of their favorites. A forged history would have clothed friends with every virtue, and would not have ventured to mar the effect designed to be produced by uncovering the vices of its most distinguished personages. Here then, is displayed the uniqueness of Scripture history. Its characters are painted in the colors of truth and nature. But such characters were never sketched by a human pencil. Moses and the other writers must have written by Divine inspiration.

The sin of idolatry, while it is the worst of which Israel was guilty, is not the only evil recorded against them—their whole history is one long story of repeated apostasy from Jehovah their God. After they had been emancipated from the bondage of Egypt and had been miraculously delivered from their cruel masters at the Red Sea, they commenced their journey towards the Promised Land.

Between them and their goal lay a march across the wilderness, and here the depravity of their hearts was fully manifested. In spite of the fact that Jehovah, by overthrowing their enemies, had plainly demonstrated that He was their God, yet no sooner was the faith of the Israelites put to the test than their hearts failed them. First, their stores of food began to give out and they feared they would perish from hunger. Trying circumstances had banished the Living God from their thoughts. They complained of their lot and murmured against Moses. Yet God did not deal with them after their sins nor reward them according to their iniquities: in mercy, He gave them bread from heaven and furnished them a daily supply of manna. But they soon became dissatisfied with the manna and lusted after the flesh pots of Egypt. Still God dealt with them in grace.

Shortly after God's intervention in giving the Israelites food to eat, which ought for ever to have closed their murmuring mouths, they pitched in Rephidim where "there was no water for the people to drink. Wherefore the people did chide with Moses, and said, Give us water that we may drink. And Moses said unto them, Why chide ye with me? wherefore do ye tempt the Lord? And the people thirsted there for water; and the people murmured against Moses, and said, Wherefore is this that thou hast brought us up out of Egypt, to kill us and our children and our cattle with thirst? And Moses cried unto the Lord, saying, What shall I do unto this people? they be almost ready to stone me." What was God's response? Did His anger consume them? Did He refuse to bear longer with such a stiff-necked people? No: "The Lord said unto Moses, Go on before the people, and take with thee of the elders of Israel; and thy rod, wherewith thou smotest the river, take in thine hand, and go. Behold, I will stand before thee there upon the rock in Horeb; and thou shalt smite the rock, and there shall come water out of it, that the people may drink" (Exod. 17).

The above incidents were but sadly typical and illustrative of Israel's general conduct. When the spies were sent out to view the Promised Land and returned and reported, ten of them magnified the difficulties which confronted them and advised the people not to attempt an occupation of Canaan; and though the remaining two faithfully reminded the Israelites that the mighty Jehovah could easily overcome all their difficulties, nevertheless, the nation listened not but heeded the word of their skeptical advisers. Time after time they provoked Jehovah, and in consequence the whole of that generation perished in the wilderness. When the succeeding generation was grown, under the leadership of Joshua they entered the Promised Land and by the aid of God overthrew many of their enemies and occupied much of their territory. But after the death of Joshua we read, "There arose another generation after them, which knew not the Lord, nor yet the works which He had done for Israel. And the children of Israel did evil in the sight of the Lord God of their fathers, which brought them out of the land of Egypt, and followed other gods, of the gods of the people that were round about them, and bowed themselves unto them, and provoked the Lord to anger. And they forsook the Lord, and served Baal and Ashtaroth" (Judge. 2:10-13). There is no need for us to follow further the fluctuating fortunes of Israel: as is well known, under the period of the judges their history was a series of returns to the Lord and subsequent departures from Him; repeated deliverances from the hands of their enemies, and then returning unfaithfulness on their part, followed by being again delivered unto their foes. Under the kings it was no better. The very first of their kings perished through his willful disobedience and apostasy; the third king, Solomon, violated God's law and married heathen women who turned his heart unto false gods. Solomon, in turn, was followed by a number of idolatrous rulers, and the path of Israel ran farther and farther away from the Lord, until He delivered them over unto Nebuchadnezzar who captured their beloved Jerusalem, destroyed their Temple, and carried away the people into captivity.

In the repeated mention which we have in the Old Testament of Israel's sins, we discover, in light as clear as day, the absolute honesty and candor of those who recorded Israel's history. No attempt whatever is made to conceal their folly, their unbelief, and their wickedness; instead, the corrupt condition of their hearts is made fully manifest, and this, by writers who belonged to, and were born of the same nation. In the whole realm of literature there is no parallel. The record of Israel's history is absolutely unique. The careful reader would at first conclude that Israel as a nation was more depraved than any other, yet further reflection will show that the inference is a false one and that the real fact is that the history of Israel has been more faithfully transmitted than that of any other nation. We mean the history of Israel as it

The Divine Inspiration of the Bible

is recorded in the Holy Scriptures, for in striking contrast thereto and in exemplification of all that we have written above, it is noteworthy that Josephus passes over in silence whatever appeared unfavorable to his nation!!

Coming now to the New Testament we begin with the character of John the Baptist and the position that he occupied. John the Baptist is presented as a most eminent personage. We are told that his birth was due to the miraculous intervention of God. We learn that he was "filled with the Holy Spirit, even from his mother's womb" (Luke 1:15). John the Baptist was himself the subject of Old Testament prediction. The office that he filled was the most honorable which ever fell to the lot of any member of Adam's race. He was the harbinger of the Messiah. He was the one who went before our Lord to prepare His way. He had the honor of baptizing the blessed Redeemer. Now where would human wisdom have placed him among the attendants of the Lord Jesus? What position would it have ascribed to him? Surely he would have been set forth as the most distinguished among our Lord's followers; surely, human wisdom would have set him at the right hand of the Savior! Yet what do we find? Instead of this, we discover that he had no familiar discourse with the Savior; instead, we find he was treated with apparent neglect; instead, we find him represented as occupying the position of a doubter who, as the result of his imprisonment, was constrained to send a message to his Master to enquire whether or not He were the promised Messiah. Had his character been the invention of forgery, nothing would have been heard of his lapse of faith. Indeed, this is so opposed to the dictates of human wisdom, that many have been shocked at the thought of ascribing doubts to the eminent forerunner of Christ, and have taxed their ingenuity to the utmost to force from the obvious meaning of the record some other and some different signification. But all these ingenuities of human sophistry are dissipated by the reply which our Lord made on the occasion of John's inquiry (Matt. 11), a reply which shows very plainly that the question was asked not for the benefit of his disciples, but because the Baptist's own heart was harassed with doubts. Again, we say that no human mind could have invented the character of John the Baptist, and the faithfulness of his biographers is another proof that the writers of the Bible were actuated by something more and something higher than the principles of human nature.

Another striking illustration of our chapter heading—one which many writers have pointed out—is the treatment the Son of God received while He tabernacled among men. For two thousand years Israel's hopes had all centered in the advent of their Messiah. The height of every Jewish woman's ambition was that she might be selected of God to have the honor of being the mother of the promised Seed. For centuries, every pious Hebrew had looked and longed for the day when He should appear who was to occupy David's throne and rule and reign in righteousness. Yet, when He did appear how was the Promised One received? "He was despised and rejected of men." "He came unto His own and His own received Him not." Those who were His brethren according to the flesh "hated" Him "without a cause." The very nation which gave Him birth and to which He ministered in infinite grace and blessing demanded that He should be crucified. The startling thing which we desire to particularly emphasize is, that the narrators of this awful tragedy are fellow countrymen of those upon whose heads rested the guilt of its perpetration. It was Jewish writers who recorded the fearful crime of the Jewish nation against their Messiah! And, we say again, that in the recording of that crime no attempt whatever is made to palliate or extenuate their wickedness; instead, it is denounced and condemned in the most uncompromising terms. Israel is openly charged with having taken and with "wicked hands" slain the "Lord of Glory." Such an honest and impartial recital of Israel's crowning sin can only be explained on the ground that what these men wrote was inspired of God.

One more illustration must suffice. After our Lord's death and resurrection, He commissioned His disciples to go forth carrying from Him a message first to His own nation and later to "every creature." This message, be it noted, was not a malediction called down upon the heads of His heartless murderers, but a proclamation of grace. It was a message of good news, of glad tidings—forgiveness was to be preached in His name to all men. How then would human wisdom suppose such a message will be received? It is further to be observed that those who were thus commissioned to carry the Gospel to the lost, were vested with power to heal the sick and to cast out demons. Surely such a beneficent ministry will meet with a universal welcome! Yet, incredible as it may appear, the Apostles of Christ met with no more appreciation than did their Master. They, too, were despised and rejected. They,

The Divine Inspiration of the Bible

too, were hated and persecuted. They, too, were ill-treated, imprisoned, and put to a shameful death. And this, not merely from the hands of the bigoted Jews, but from the cultured Greeks and from the democratic and freedom loving Romans as well. Though these Apostles brought blessing, they themselves were cursed; though they sought to emancipate men from the thraldom of sin and Satan, yet they were themselves captured and thrown into prison; though they healed the sick and raised the dead, they suffered martyrdom. Surely it is apparent to every impartial mind that the New Testament is no mere human invention; and surely it is evident from the honesty of its writers in so faithfully portraying the enmity of the carnal mind against God, that their productions can only be accounted for on the ground that they spoke and wrote "not of themselves," but "as they were moved by the Holy Spirit" (2 Pet. 1:21).

Arthur W. Pink

CHAPTER FOUR
THE CHARACTER OF ITS TEACHINGS EVIDENCES THE DIVINE AUTHORSHIP OF THE BIBLE

Take its teachings about God Himself. What does the Bible teach us about God? It declares that He is Eternal: "Before the mountains were brought forth, or ever Thou hadst formed the earth and the world, even from everlasting to everlasting, Thou are God" (Ps. 90:2). It reveals the fact that He is Infinite: "But will God indeed dwell on the earth? Behold, the heaven and heaven of heavens cannot contain Thee" (1 Kings 8:27). Vast as we know the universe to be, it has its bounds; but we must go beyond them to conceive of God—"Canst thou by searching find out God? Canst thou find out the Almighty unto perfection? It is as high as heaven; what canst thou do? deeper than hell; what canst thou know? The measure thereof is longer than the earth, and broader than the sea" (Job 11:7-9). It makes mention of His Sovereignty: "Remember the former things of old: for I am God, and there is none else; I am God, and there is none like Me, declaring the end from the beginning, and from ancient times the things that are not yet done, saying, My counsel shall stand, and I will do all My pleasure" (Isa. 46: 9-10). It affirms that He is Omnipotent: "Behold I am the Lord, the God of all flesh: is there anything too hard for Me?" (Jer. 32:27). It intimates that He is Omniscient: "Great is our Lord, and of great power: His understanding is infinite" (Ps. 147:5). It teaches that He is Omnipresent: "Can any hide himself in secret places that I shall not see him? saith the Lord. Do not I fill heaven and earth? saith the Lord" (Jer. 23:24). It declares that He is Immutable: "The same yesterday, and today, and forever" (Heb. 13:8). Yea, that with Him "is no variableness, neither shadow of turning" (James 1:17). It reveals that He is "The Judge of all the earth" (Gen. 18:25) and that everyone shall yet have to "give an account of himself to God"

The Divine Inspiration of the Bible

(Rom. 14:12). It announces that He is inflexibly just in all His dealings so that He can by "no means clear the guilty" (Num. 14:18); that all will be judged "according to their works" (Rev. 20:12), and that they shall reap whatsoever they have sown (Gal 6:7). It reveals the fact that He is absolutely holy, dwelling in light inaccessible. So holy that even the seraphim have to veil their faces in His presence (Isa. 6:2). So holy that the heavens are not clean in His sight (Job 15:15). So holy that the best of men when face to face with their Maker, have to cry, "I abhor myself" (Job 42:6); "Woe is me! For I am undone" (Isa. 6:5). Such a delineation of Deity is as far beyond man's conception as the heavens are above the earth. No man, and no number of men, ever invented such a God as this. Ransack the libraries of the ancient, examine the musings of the mystics, study the religions of the heathen and nothing will be found which can for a moment be compared with the sublime and exalted description of God's character which is furnished by the Bible.

The teachings of the Bible about man are unique. Unlike all other books in the world, the Bible condemns man and all his doings. It never eulogizes his wisdom, nor praises his achievements. On the contrary, it declares that "every man at his best state is altogether vanity" (Ps 39:5). Instead of teaching that man is a noble character, evolving heavenwards, it tells him that all his righteousnesses (his best works) are as "filthy rags," that he is a lost sinner, incapable of bettering his condition; that he is deserving only of Hell.

The picture which the Scriptures give of man is deeply humiliating and entirely different from all which are drawn by human pencils. The Word of God describes the state of the natural man in the following language: —"There is none righteous, no, not one. There is none that understandeth, there is none that seeketh after God. They are all gone out of the way, they are together become unprofitable. There is none that doeth good, no, not one. Their throat is an open sepulcher; with their tongues they have used deceit; the poison of asps is under their lips; whose mouth is full of cursing and bitterness. Their feet are swift to shed blood: destruction and misery are in their ways: and the way of peace have they not known. There is no fear of God before their eyes" (Rom. 3:10-18).

Instead of making Satan the source of all the black crimes of which we are guilty, the Bible declares, "For from within, out of the heart of man proceed evil thoughts, adulteries, fornications, murders, thefts, covetousness, wickedness, deceit, lasciviousness, an evil eye, blasphemy, pride, foolishness: all these evil things come from within and defile the man" (Mark 7:21-23). Such a conception of man—so different from man's own ideas, and so humiliating to his proud heart—never could have emanated from man himself. "The heart is deceitful above all things and desperately wicked" (Jer. 17:9) is a concept that never originated in any human mind.

The teachings of the Bible about the world are unique. In nothing perhaps are the teachings of Scripture and the writings of man at such variance as they are at this point. Using the term as meaning the world-system in contradistinction to the earth, what is the direction of man's thoughts concerning the same? Man thinks highly of the world, for he regards it as his world. It is that which his labors have produced and he looks upon it with satisfaction and pride. He boasts that "the world is growing better." He declares that the world is becoming more civilized and more humanized. Man's thoughts upon this subject have been well summarized by the poet in the familiar language—"God is in heaven: All's well with the world." But what saith the Scriptures? Upon this subject, too, we discover that God's thoughts are very different from ours. The Bible uniformly condemns the world and speaks of it as a thing of evil. We shall not attempt to quote every passage which does this, but shall merely single out a few specimen Scriptures.

"If the world hate you, ye know that it hated Me before it hated you. If ye were of the world, the world would love his own: but because ye are not of the world, but I have chosen you out of the world, therefore the world hateth you" (John 15:18-19). This passage teaches that the world hates both Christ and His followers. "The wisdom of this world is foolishness with God" (1 Cor 3:19). Certainly no uninspired pen wrote these words. "Ye adulterers and adulteresses, know ye not that the friendship of the world is enmity with God? Whosoever therefore will be a friend of the world is the enemy of God" (James 4:4). Here again we learn that the world is an evil thing, condemned by God, and to be shunned by His children. "Love not the world, neither the things that are in the world. If any man love the world, the love of the Father is not in him. For all that is in the world, the lust of the flesh, and the lust of the eyes, and the pride of life, is not of the Father, but is of the world" (1 John 2:15-16). Here we have a definition of the world: it is all that is opposed to the Father—opposed in its principles

The Divine Inspiration of the Bible

and philosophy, its maxims and methods, its aims and ambitions, its trend and its end "And the whole world lieth in the Evil One" (1 John 5:19, R.V.). Here we learn why it is that the world hates Christ and His followers; why its wisdom is foolishness with God; why it is condemned by God and must be shunned by His children—it is under the dominion of that old serpent, the devil, whom Scripture specifically denominates "The prince of this world."

The teachings of the Bible about sin is unique. Man regards sin as a misfortune and ever seeks to minimize its enormity. In these days, sin is referred to as ignorance, as a necessary stage in man's development. By others, sin is looked upon as a mere negation, the opposite of good; while Mrs. Eddy and her followers went so far as to deny its existence altogether. But the Bible, unlike every other book, strips man of all excuse and emphasizes his culpability. In the Bible sin is never palliated or extenuated, but from first to last the Holy Scriptures insist upon its enormity and heinousness. The Word of God declares that "sin is very grievous" (Gen. 18:20) and that our sins provoke God to anger (1 Kings 16:2). It speaks of the "deceitfulness of sin" (Heb. 3:13) and insists that sin is "exceedingly sinful" (Rom 7:13). It declares that all sin is sin against God (Ps. 51:4) and against His Christ (1 Cor. 8:12). It regards our sins as being "as scarlet" and "red like crimson" (Isa. 1:18). It declares that sin is more than an act, it is an attitude. It affirms that sin is more than a non-compliance with God's law—it is rebellion against the One who gave the law . It teaches that "sin is lawlessness" (1 John 3:4, R. V.), which means that sin is spiritual anarchy, open defiance against the Almighty. Moreover, it singles out no particular class; it condemns all alike. It announces that "all have sinned and come short of the glory of God," that "there is none righteous, no, not one" (Rom. 3). Did man ever write such an indictment against himself? What human mind ever invented such a description of sin as that discovered in the Bible? Whoever would have imagined that sin was such a vile and dreadful thing in the sight of God that nothing but the precious blood of His own beloved Son could make an atonement for it!

The teaching of the Bible about the punishment of sin is unique. A defective view of sin necessarily leads to an inadequate conception of what is due sin. Minimize the gravity and enormity of sin and you must proportionately reduce the sentence which it deserves. Many are crying out today against the justice of the eternal punishment of sin. They complain that the penalty does not fit the crime. They argue that it is unrighteous for a sinner to suffer eternally in consequence of a short life span of wrong-doing. But even in this world it is not the length of time which it takes to commit the crime which determines the severity of the sentence. Many a man has suffered a life term of imprisonment for a crime which required only a few minutes for its perpetration. Apart, however, from this consideration, eternal punishment is just if sin be looked at from God's viewpoint. But this is just what the majority of men refuse to do. They look at sin and its deserts solely from the human side. One reason why the Bible was written was to correct our ideas and views about sin, to teach us what an unspeakably awful and vile thing it is, to show us sin as God sees it. For one single sin Adam and Eve were banished from Eden. For one single sin Canaan and all his posterity were cursed. For a single sin Korah and his company went down alive into the pit. For one single sin Moses was debarred from entering the Promised Land. For a single sin Achan and his family were stoned to death. For a single sin Elisha's servant was smitten with leprosy. For a single sin Ananias and Sapphira were cut off out of the land of the living. Why? To teach us what an infinite evil it is to revolt against the thrice holy God. We repeat, that did men but see the terribleness of sin—did they but see that it was sin that put to a shameful death the Lord of Glory—then they would realize that nothing short of eternal punishment would meet the demands which justice has upon sinners.

But the great majority of men do not see the meetness or justice of eternal punishment; on the contrary, they cry out against it. In lands which were not illumined by the Old Testament Scriptures, where there existed any belief in a future life, it was held that at death the wicked either passed through some temporary suffering for remedial and purifying purposes or else they were annihilated. Even in Christendom, where the Word of God has held a prominent and public place for centuries, the great bulk of the people do not believe in eternal punishment. They argue that God is too merciful and kind to ban one of His own creatures to endless misery. Yea, not a few of the Lord's own people are afraid to take the solemn teachings of the Scriptures on this subject at their face value. It is therefore evident that had the Bible been written by uninspired men; had it been a mere human composition, it certainly would

The Divine Inspiration of the Bible

not have taught the eternal and conscious torment of all who die out of Christ. The fact that the Bible does so teach is conclusive proof that it was written by men who spoke not of themselves, but as they were "moved by the Holy Spirit."

The teachings of God's Word upon eternal punishment are as clear and explicit as they are solemn and awful. They declare that the doom of the Christ rejector is a conscious, never-ending, indescribable torment. The Bible depicts the place of punishment as a realm where the "worm dieth not" and "the fire is not quenched" (Mark 9:48). It speaks of it as a lake of fire and brimstone (Rev. 20:10), where even a drop of water is denied the agonized sufferer (Luke 16:24). It declares that "the smoke of their torment ascendeth up for ever and ever: and they have no rest day nor night" (Rev. 14:11). It represents the world of the lost as a scene into which penetrates no light—"the blackness of darkness forever" (Jude 1: 13) —a doom alleviated by no ray of hope. In short, the portion of the lost will be unbearable, yet it will have to be borne, and borne forever. What mortal mind conceived of such a fate? Such a conception is too repugnant and repulsive to the human heart to have had its birth on the earth.

The teachings of the Bible about Salvation from Sin is unique. Man's thoughts about salvation, like every other subject which engages his mind are defective and deficient. Hence the force of the admonition—"Let the wicked forsake his way and the unrighteous man his thoughts" (Isa. 55:7). In the first place, left to himself, man fails to realize his need of salvation. In the pride of his heart he imagines that he is sufficient in himself, and through the darkening of his understanding by sin he fails to comprehend his ruined and lost condition. Like the self-righteous Pharisee, he thanks God that he is not as other men, that he is morally the superior of the savage or the criminal, and refuses to believe that so far as his standing before God is concerned there is "no difference." It is not until the Holy Spirit deals with him that man is constrained to cry, "God be merciful to me a sinner."

In the second place man is ignorant of the way of salvation. Even when man has been brought to the place where he recognizes that he is not prepared to meet God, and that if he died in his present state he would be eternally lost; even then he has no right conception of the remedy. Being ignorant of God's righteousness he goes about to establish his own righteousness. He supposes that he must make some personal reparation for his past wrongdoings, that he must work for his salvation, do something to merit the esteem of God, and thus win heaven as a reward. The highest concept of man's mind is that of merit. To him salvation is a wage to be earned, a crown to be coveted, a prize to be won. The proof of this is to be seen in the fact that even when pardon and life are presented as a free gift, the universal tendency, at first, is to regard it as being "too good to be true." Yet, such is the plain teaching of God's Word—"For by grace are ye saved through faith; and that not of yourselves: it is the gift of God: not of works; lest any man should boast" (Eph. 2:8-9). And again—"Not by works of righteousness which we have done, but according to His mercy He saved us" (Titus 3:5).

If it is true that man left to himself would never have fully realized his need of salvation, and would never have discovered that it was by grace through faith and not of works, how much less would the human mind have been capable of rising to the level of what God's Word teaches about the nature of salvation and the glorious and marvelous destiny of the saved! Who would have thought that the Maker and Ruler of the universe should lay hold of poor, fallen, depraved men and women and lifting them out of the miry clay should make them His own sons and daughters, and should seat them at His own table! Who would ever have suggested that those who deserve naught but everlasting shame and contempt, should be made "heirs of God and joint-heirs with Christ"! Who would have dreamed that beggars should be lifted from the dunghill of sin and made to sit together with Christ in heavenly places! Who would have imagined that the corrupted offspring of disobedient Adam should be exalted to a position higher than that occupied by the unfallen angels! Who would have dared to affirm that one day we shall be "made like Christ" and "be forever with the Lord"! Such concepts were as far beyond the reach of the highest human intellect as they were of the rudest savage. "But as it is written, eye hath not seen, nor ear heard, neither have entered into the heart of man, the things which God hath prepared for them that love Him. But God hath revealed them unto us by His Spirit: for the Spirit searcheth all things, yea, the deep things of God" (1 Cor. 2:9-10).

Again we ask, what human intellect could have devised a means whereby God could be just and yet merciful, merciful and yet just?

The Divine Inspiration of the Bible

What mortal mind would ever have dreamed of a free and full salvation, bestowed on hell-deserving sinners, "without money and without price"! And what flight of carnal imagination would ever have conceived of the Son of God Himself being "made sin" for us and dying the Just for the unjust?

The teaching of the Bible concerning the Savior of sinners is unique. The description which the Scriptures furnish of the Person, the Character, and the Work of the Lord Jesus Christ is without anything that approaches a parallel in the whole realm of literature. It is easier to suppose that man could create a world than to believe he invented the character of our adorable Redeemer. Given a piece of machinery that is delicate, complex, exact in all its movements, and we know it must be the product of a competent mechanic. Given a work of art that is beautiful, symmetrical, original, and we know it must be the product of a master artist. None but an Angelo could have designed Saint Peter's; none but a Raphael could have painted the "transfiguration;" none but a Milton could have written a "Paradise Lost." And, none but the Holy Spirit could have produced the peerless portrait of the Lord Jesus which we find in the Gospels. In Christ all excellences combine. Here is one of the many respects in which He differs from all other Bible characters. In each of the great heroes of Scripture some trait stands out with peculiar distinctness—Noah, faithful testimony; Abraham, faith in God; Isaac, submission to his father; Joseph, love for his brethren; Moses, unselfishness and meekness; Joshua, courage and leadership; Job, fortitude and patience; Daniel, fidelity to God; Paul, zeal in service; John, spiritual discernment—but in the Lord Jesus every grace is found. Moreover, in Him all these perfections were properly poised and balanced. He was meek yet regal; He was gentle yet fearless; He was compassionate yet just; He was submissive yet authoritative; He was Divine yet human; add to these, the fact that He was absolutely "without sin" and His uniqueness becomes apparent. Nowhere in all the writings of antiquity is there to be found the presentation of such a peerless and wondrous character.

Not only is the portrayal of Christ's character without any rival, but the teaching of the Bible concerning His Person and Work is also utterly incredible on any other basis save that they are part of a Divine revelation. Who would have dared to imagine the Creator and Upholder of the universe taking upon Himself the form of a servant and being made in the likeness of men? Who would have conceived the idea of the Lord of Glory being born in a manger? Who would have dreamed of the Object of angelic worship becoming so poor that he had not where to lay His head? Who would have declared that the One before whom the seraphim veil their faces should be led as a lamb to the slaughter, should have suffered His own blessed face to be defiled with the vile spittle of man, and should permit the creatures of His hand to scourge and buffet Him? Whoever would have conceived of Emmanuel becoming obedient unto death, even the death of the Cross!

Here then is an argument which the simplest can grasp. The Scriptures contain their own evidence that they are Divinely inspired. Every page of Holy Writ is stamped with Jehovah's autograph. The uniqueness of its teachings demonstrates the uniqueness of its Source. The teachings of the Scriptures about God Himself, about man, about the world, about sin, about eternal punishment, about salvation, about the Lord Jesus Christ, are proof that the Bible is not the product of any man or any number of men, but is in truth a revelation from God.

CHAPTER FIVE
THE FULFILLED PROPHECIES OF THE BIBLE BESPEAK THE OMNISCIENCE OF ITS AUTHOR

In Isaiah 41:21-23 we have what is probably the most remarkable challenge to be found in the Bible. "Produce your cause, saith the Lord; bring forth your strong reasons, saith the King of Jacob. Let them bring them forth, and show us what shall happen; let them show the former things, what they be, that we may consider them, and know the latter end of them; or declare us things for to come. Show the things that are to come hereafter, that we may know that ye are gods." This Scripture has both a negative and a positive value: negatively it suggests an infallible criterion by which we may test the claims of religious impostors; positively, it calls attention to an unanswerable argument for the truthfulness of God's Word. Jehovah bids the prophets of false faiths to successfully predict events lying in the far distant future and their success or failure will show whether or not they are gods or merely pretenders and deceivers. On the other hand, the demonstrated fact that God alone grasps the ages and in His Word declares the end from the beginning, shows that he is God and that Scriptures are His Inspired Revelation to mankind.

Again and again men have attempted to predict future events but always with the most disastrous failure, the anticipations of the most far-seeing and the precautions of the wisest are mocked repeatedly by the bitter irony of events. Man stands before an impenetrable wall of darkness, he is unable to foresee the events of even the next hour. None knows what a day may bring forth. To the finite mind the future is filled with unknown possibilities. How then can we explain the hundreds of detailed prophecies in the Scriptures which have been literally fulfilled to the letter, hundreds of years after they were uttered? How can we account for the fact that the Bible successfully foretold hundreds, and in some instances thousands of years beforehand, the History of the Jews, the Course of the Gentiles, and the Experiences of the Church? The most conservative of critics, and the most daring assailants of God's Word are compelled to acknowledge that all the Books of the Old Testament were written hundreds of years before the incarnation of our Lord, hence, the actual and accurate fulfillment of these prophecies can only be explained on the hypothesis that "Prophecy came not at any time by the will of men: but holy men of God, spoke, moved by the Holy Ghost."

The Inspirer of the Scriptures has told us that "We have also a more sure word of prophecy; where unto ye do well that ye take heed as unto a light that shineth in a dark place" (2 Pet. 1:19). In the limited space at our command we shall appeal to but a few from among the many fulfilled prophecies of God's Word, and shall limit ourselves to those which have reference to the Person and Work of the Lord Jesus Christ. The cumulative force of these will be sufficient, we trust, to convince any impartial inquirer that none other but the mind of God could have disclosed the future and unveiled beforehand far distant events.

"The testimony of Jesus is the Spirit of Prophecy." The Lamb of God is the one great object and subject of the Prophetic Word. In Genesis 3:15 we have the first word about the Coming of Christ. Speaking to the serpent, Jehovah said, "And I will put enmity between thee and the woman, and between thy seed and her seed; it shall bruise thy head, and thou shall bruise His heel." Note that the Coming One was to be the "woman's seed," the Miraculous Character of our Lord's Birth being thus foretold four thousand years before He was born at Bethlehem!

In Genesis 22:18 we have the second distinct Messianic prophecy. Unto Abraham, the angel of the Lord declared, "And in thy seed shall all the nations of the earth be blessed." Not only was the Savior of sinners to be human as well as Divine, not only was He to be the "woman's" seed, but in the above Scripture it was declared that He should be a descendant of Abraham—an Israelite. How this was fulfilled we may see by a reference to the first verse in the New Testament, where we are told (Matt. 1:1) that Jesus Christ was "The Son of David, the son of Abraham."

But still further was the compass narrowed down, for we have intimated in the Old Testament Scriptures the very tribe from which the Messiah was to issue—our Lord was to come of the Tribe of Judah (the "kingly" tribe). He was to be a descendant of David. Nathan the prophet was commanded by God to go and say to David, "I will set up thy seed after thee, which shall proceed out of thy bowels, and I will establish His kingdom. He shall build an house for My name, and I will establish the throne of His kingdom forever" (2 Sam. 7:12-13). And again, in Psalm 132:11 David declares concerning the promised Messiah, "The Lord hath sworn in truth unto David; (He will not turn from it) Of the fruit of thy body will I set upon thy throne.

Not only was our Lord's nationality defined hundreds of years before His incarnation, but the very place of His birth was also given. In Micah 5:2 we are informed, "But thou, Bethlehem Ephratah, though thou be little among the thousands of Judah, but out of thee shall He come forth unto Me that is to be Ruler in Israel; whose goings forth have been from of old, from the days of eternity." Christ was to be born in Bethlehem, and not only in one of the several villages which bore that name in Palestine, but Bethlehem of Judea was to be the birth-place of the world's Redeemer; and though Mary was a native of Nazareth (far distant from Bethlehem) yet through the providence of God, His Word was literally fulfilled by His Son being born in Bethlehem of Judea.

Further, the very time of Messiah's appearing was given through both Jacob and Daniel (see Gen. 49:10 and Daniel 9:24-26). Now in order to appreciate the force of these marvelous, super-natural prophecies, let the reader seek to foretell the nationality, place and time of the birth of someone who shall be born in the twenty-fifth century A. D., and then he will realize that none but a man inspired and informed by God Himself could perform such an otherwise impossible feat.

So definite and distinct were the Old Testament prophecies respecting the Birth of Christ, that the hope of Israel became the Messianic Hope; all their expectations were centered in the coming of the Messiah. It is therefore the more remarkable that their sacred Scriptures should contain another set of prophecies which predicted that He should be despised by His own nation and rejected by His own kinsmen. We can only now call attention to one of the prophecies which declared that the Messiah of Israel should be slighted and scorned by His brethren according to the flesh.

In Isaiah 53:2-3 we read, "And when we (Israel) shall see Him, there is no beauty that we should desire Him. He is despised and rejected of men; a Man of sorrows, and acquainted with grief; and we hid as it were our faces from Him; He was despised, and we esteemed Him not!" We pause here for a moment to enlarge upon this strange and striking phenomenon.

For more than fifteen centuries the Coming of the Messiah had been the one great national Hope of Israel. From the cradle the sons of Abraham were taught to pray and long for His advent. The eagerness with which they awaited the appearing of the Star of Jacob is absolutely without parallel in the history of any other nation. How then can we account for the fact that when He did come He was despised and rejected? How can we explain the fact that side by side with the intense longing for the manifestation of their King, one of their own prophets foretold that when He did appear men would hide their faces from Him and esteem Him not? Finally, what explanation have we to offer for the fact that such things were predicted centuries before He came to this earth and that they were literally fulfilled to the very letter? As another has said, "No prediction could have seemed more improbable, and yet none ever received a sadder and more complete fulfillment."

We pass on now to those predictions which have reference to the death of our Lord. If it was wonderful that an Israelitish prophet should foretell the rejection of the Messiah by His own nation, what shall we say to the fact that the Old Testament Scriptures prophesied in detail concerning the manner or form of His death? Yet again and again we find this to be the case! Let us examine a few typical instances.

First, it was intimated that our Lord should be betrayed and sold for the price of a common slave. In Zechariah 11:12 we read, "So they weighed for My price thirty pieces of silver." Who was it that was able to declare, centuries before the event came to pass, the exact amount that Judas should receive for his dastardly deed? In Isaiah 53:7 we have another line in this marvelous picture which human wisdom could not possibly have supplied—"He is brought as a lamb to the slaughter, and as a sheep before her shearers is dumb, so He opened not His mouth." Who could have foreseen this most unusual sight, of a prisoner standing before his judges with his life at stake, yet attempting and offering no defense? Yet this is precisely what did happen in connection with our Lord, for we are told in Mark 15:5, "But Jesus yet answered nothing; so that Pilate marveled." Again; who was it that knew seven hundred years before the greatest tragedy of human history was enacted that the Son of God, the King of the Jews, the gentlest and meekest Man who ever trod our earth, should be scourged and spat upon? Yet such an experience was foretold: "I gave My back to the smiters, and My cheeks to them that plucked off the hair: I hid not My face from shame and spitting" (Isa. 50:6).

Further; the form of capital punishment reserved for Jewish criminals was "stoning to death," and in David's time the experience of "crucifixion" was entirely unknown, yet we find in Psalm 22:16 that Israel's king was inspired to write, "They pierced My hands and My feet!" Again; what human foresight could have seen that in His thirst-agonies upon the cross our Lord should be given gall and vinegar to drink? Yet it was declared a thousand years before the Lord of Glory was nailed to the tree that, "They gave Me also gall for My meat; and in My thirst they gave Me vinegar to drink." (Ps. 69:21). Finally; we ask, how could David foretell, unless he was inspired by the Holy Spirit, that our Lord should be taunted by His enemies and challenged to come down from the Cross? Yet in Psalm 22:7-8 we read, "All they that see Me laugh Me to scorn: they shoot out the lip, they shake the head, saying, He trusted on the Lord that He would deliver Him: let Him deliver Him, seeing He delighted in Him." Such examples as the above might be multiplied indefinitely, but sufficient illustrations have already been given to warrant us in saying that the fulfilled prophecies of the Bible bespeak the omniscience of its Author.

Were it necessary, and had we the space at our command, scores of additional fulfilled prophecies relating to the History of Israel, the Course of the Gentiles, and the Experiences of the Church—prophecies just as definite, accurate, and remarkable as those relating to the Person of the Lord Jesus Christ—could be given, but our present limits and purpose forbid us so doing.

Having examined a few of the startling prophecies which treat of the Birth and Death of our Savior, it now only remains for us to apply in a word the significance of this argument. Many have read over these Scriptures before and perhaps have regarded them as being wonderfully descriptive of the Advent and Passion of Jesus Christ, but how many have carefully weighed the fact that each of these Scriptures were in indisputable existence more than five hundred years before our Lord came to this earth?

Man is unable to accurately predict events which are but twenty-four hours distant; only the Divine Mind could have foretold the future, centuries before it came to be. Hence, we affirm with the utmost confidence, that the hundreds of fulfilled prophecies in the Bible attest and demonstrate the truth that the Scriptures are the inspired, infallible, inerrant Word of God.

CHAPTER SIX
THE TYPICAL SIGNIFICANCE OF THE SCRIPTURES DECLARE THEIR DIVINE AUTHORSHIP

"In the volume of the Book it is written of Me" (Heb. 10:7). Christ is the Key to the Scriptures. Said He, "Search the Scriptures. . .they are they which testify of Me." (John 5:39), and the "Scriptures" to which He had reference, were not the four Gospels for they were not then written, but the writings of Moses and the prophets. The Old Testament Scriptures then are something more than a compilation of historical records, something more than a system of social and religious legislation, something more than a code of ethics. The Old Testament Scriptures are fundamentally a stage on which is shown forth in vivid symbolism and ritualism the whole plan of redemption. The events recorded in the Old Testament were actual occurrences, yet they were also typical prefigurations. Throughout the Old Testament dispensations God caused to be shadowed forth in parabolic representation the whole work of redemption by means of a constant and vivid appeal to the senses. This was in full accord with a fundamental law in the economy of God. Nothing is brought to maturity at once. As it is in the natural world, so it is in the spiritual: there is first the blade, then the ear, and then the full corn in the ear. Concerning the Person and work of the Lord Jesus, God first gave a series of pictorial representations, later a large number of specific prophecies, and last of all, when the fullness of time was come, God sent forth His own Son.

It is failure to discern the typical import of the Old Testament Scriptures which has caused so great a part of them to be slighted by so many readers of the Bible. To multitudes of people the Pentateuch is little more than a compilation of effete and meaningless ceremonial rites, and if there is nothing in them more excellent than their outward semblance, then, surely, it is passing strange that they should find a place in the Word of God. Take Christ out of Old Testament ritual and you are left with nothing but the dry and empty shell of a nut. It is therefore a matter of small surprise that those who see so little of Christ in the Old Testament Scriptures should undervalue the instruction and edification to be derived from every part of them, and that they entertain such degrading ideas of their inspiration. Deny that there is a spiritual meaning in all the laws and customs of the Israelites and what food for the soul can be gathered from a study of them? Deny that they are so many typical representations of Christ and His Sacrifice for sin and you cast reproach on the name and wisdom of God by suggesting that He instituted the carnal ordinances, the cumbrous ceremonies, the propitiations by sacrifice of animals, which are recorded in the opening Books of the Bible.

The typical import and the spiritual value of the Jewish economy, both as a whole and in its many parts, is expressly affirmed in the New Testament. The Apostle Paul, when referring to the narratives and events recorded in the Old Testament, declares that, "Whatsoever things were written aforetime were written for our learning" (Rom. 15:4). Later, when making mention of Israel's exodus from Egypt and their journey through the wilderness, he affirms, "Now these things were our examples" and "Now all these things happened unto them for ensamples: (marg. "types") and they are written for our admonition" (1 Cor. 10:6-11). Again; when commenting upon, and while expounding the spiritual significance of the Tabernacle, he declares that it was "the example and shadow of heavenly things" (Heb. 8:5). In the next chapter he declares, "The Tabernacle...was a figure for the time then present" (Heb. 9:8-9) and in Hebrews 10 he states, "The law" had "a shadow of good things to come" (10:1). From these declarations it is evident that God Himself caused the Tabernacle to be erected exactly according to the pattern which He had showed Moses, for the express purpose that it should be a type for symbolizing heavenly things. Hence it becomes our privilege and bounden duty to seek by the help of the Holy Spirit to ascertain the meaning of the types of the Old Testament.

In addition to the express declarations of the New Testament quoted above, there are a number of additional passages which also teach the same thing. John the Baptist hailed our Savior as

The Divine Inspiration of the Bible

"The Lamb of God which taketh away the sin of the world," that is, as the great Antitype of the sacrificial lambs of Old Testament ritual. In His discourse with Nicodemus our Lord alluded to the lifting up of the Brazen Serpent in the wilderness as a type of His own lifting up on the Cross. Writing to the Corinthians the Apostle Paul said, "Christ our Passover is sacrificed for us" (1 Cor. 5:7), thus signifying that Exodus 12 pointed forward to the Lord Jesus. Writing to the Galatians the same Apostle makes mention of the history of Abraham, his wives and his children, and then states "which things are an allegory" (Gal. 4:24). Now there are many brethren who will own the typical significance of these things, but who refuse to acknowledge that anything else in the Old Testament has a typical meaning save those which are expressly interpreted in the New. But this we conceive to be a mistake and to place a limit upon the scope and value of the Word of God. Rather let us regard those Old Testament types which are expounded in the New Testament as samples of others which are not explained. Are there no more prophecies in the Old Testament than those which, in the New Testament, are said to be "fulfilled"? Assuredly. Then let us admit the same concerning the types.

Several volumes would be filled were we to dwell upon everything in the Old Testament which has a typical meaning and spiritual application. All we can now attempt is to single out a few illustrations as samples, leaving our readers to pursue further this entrancing study for themselves.

The very first chapter of Genesis is rich in its spiritual contents. Not only does it give us the only reliable and authentic account of the creation of this world, but it also reveals God's order in the work of the new creation. In Genesis 1:1 we have the original or primitive creation—"in the beginning". From the next verse we infer that some dreadful calamity followed. The handiwork of God was marred, "the earth became (not "was") without form and void" —a desolate waste and empty ruin. The earth was submerged. A scene of dreariness and death is introduced—"and darkness was upon the face of the deep." Not only was this the history of the earth, but it was also the history of man. In the beginning he was created by God—created in the image and likeness of his Maker. But a terrible calamity followed. An enemy appeared on the scene. The heart of the creature was seduced, unbelief and disobedience being the consequence. Man fell, and awful was his fall. God's image was broken: human nature was ruined by sin: desolation and death took the place of God's likeness and life. In consequence of his sin, man's mind was blinded and darkness rested upon the face of his understanding.

Next, we read in Genesis 1, of the work reconstruction. The order followed is profoundly significant—"The Spirit of God moved upon the face of the waters. And God said, Let there be light: and there was light" (vs. 3-4). The parallel holds good in regeneration. In the work of the new birth which is performed within the darkened and spiritually dead sinner, the Spirit of God is the prime mover, convicting the soul of its lost and ruined condition and revealing the need of the appointed Savior. The instrument that He employs is the written Word, the Word of God, and in every genuine conversion God says, "Let there be light," and there is light. "For God, who commanded the light to shine out of darkness, hath shined in our hearts, to give the light of the knowledge of the glory of God in the face of Jesus Christ" (2 Cor. 4:6). The parallel might be followed much further, but sufficient has been said to show that beneath the actual history of Genesis 1 may be discerned by the anointed eye the spiritual history of the believer's new creation, and as such it bears the stamp of its Divine Author and evidences the fact that the opening chapter of the Bible is no mere human compilation.

In the coats of skin with which the Lord God clothed our first parents we have an incident that is full of spiritual instruction and which could never have been invented by man. To obtain these skins life had to be taken, blood had to be shed, the innocent (animals) must die in the place of Adam and Eve who were guilty, so as to provide a covering for them. Thus, the Gospel truths of redemption by blood-shedding and salvation through a substitutionary sacrifice, were preached in Eden. Be it noted that man did not have to provide a covering for himself any more than the "prodigal son" did, nor were they asked to clothe themselves any more than was he: in the one case we read, "The Lord God made coats of skins and clothed them" (Gen. 3:21), and in the other the command was, "Bring forth the best robe, and put it on him" (Luke 15:22), and both speak of "the robe of righteousness" (Isa. 61:10) which is furnished in Christ.

In the offerings which Cain and Abel presented to the Lord, and in the response which they met with, we discover a foreshadowing

The Divine Inspiration of the Bible

of New testament truths. Abel brought of the firstlings of the flock with their fat. He recognized that he was alienated from God and could not draw nigh to Him without a suitable offering. He saw that his own life was forfeited through sin, that justice clamored for his death, and that his only hope lay in another (a lamb) dying in his stead. By faith Abel presented his bloody offering to God and it was accepted. On the other hand, Cain refused to take the place of a lost sinner before God. He refused to acknowledge that death was his due. He refused to place his confidence in a sacrificial substitute. He brought as an offering to God the fruits of the ground—the product of his own labors and in consequence, his offering was rejected. Thus, at the commencement of human history we have shown forth the fact that salvation is by grace through faith and altogether apart from works (Eph. 2: 8-9).

In the great Deluge and the ark in which Noah and his house found shelter, we have a typification of great spiritual verities. From them we learn that God takes cognizance of the doings of His creatures; that He is holy and sin is abhorrent to Him; that His righteousness requires Him to punish sin and destroy sinners. Yet, here also we learn that in judgment God remembers mercy, that He has no pleasure in the death of the wicked; that His grace provides a refuge if only His sinful creatures will avail themselves of His provision. Yet only in one place can deliverance from the Divine wrath be found. In the ark alone is safety and security. And, in like manner, today, there is only one Savior for sinners, and that is the Lord Jesus Christ, "Neither is there salvation in any other: for there is none other name under heaven given among men, whereby we must be saved" (Act 4:12).

In the deliverance of Israel from Egypt and their wilderness journey we see portrayed the history of God's people in the present dispensation. We, too, were living in a world "without God and without hope." We, too, were in bondage to the cruel taskmasters of sin and Satan. We, too, were in imminent danger of falling beneath the sword of the avenging Angel of Justice. But, for us, too, a way of escape was provided. For us, too, a Lamb was slain. Unto us, too, was given the precious promise, "When I see the blood I will pass over you" (Exod. 12:13). And we, too, were redeemed by Almighty power and were "delivered from the power of darkness and translated into the kingdom of God's dear Son" (Col. 1:13)

After our exodus from Egypt there lies before us a pilgrim journey through a barren and hostile wilderness as we journey toward the Promised Land. We have to pass through a strange country and meet with enemy forces, that we are unable to overcome in our own strength. For these tasks our own resources—the things we brought with us out of Egypt—are altogether inadequate, and thus we, too, are cast upon the sufficiency of Israel's God. And blessed be His name, ample provision is made for us and grace is furnished for every need. For us there is heavenly manna in the exceeding great and precious promises of God. For us there comes water out of the Smitten Rock in the person of the Holy Spirit (John 7:38-39) who refreshes our souls by taking of the things of Christ and showing them unto us and who strengthens us with might in the inner man. For us too, there is a pillar of cloud and fire to guide us by day and by night in the Holy Scriptures which are a lamp unto our feet and a light unto our path. For us, too, there is One to counsel and direct us, to intercede for us and help us overcome our Amalekites in the Captain of our salvation who has said, "Lo, I am with you always, even unto the end." And, at the close of our pilgrimage we shall enter a fairer land than that which flowed with milk and honey for we have been begotten "to an inheritance incorruptible and undefiled, and that faded not away, reserved in heaven" for us.

Let the careful and impartial reader weigh thoroughly what has been said above, and surely it is evident that the numerous resemblances between the story of Israel and the spiritual history of God's children in this dispensation cannot be so many coincidences, and can only be accounted for on the ground that the writings of Moses were inspired by the Living God.

The history of Israel in Canaan as the professed people of God corresponds with the history of the professing church in the New Testament dispensation. After Moses, the one who led Israel out from their Egyptian bondage, came Joshua who led Israel in their conquest of Canaan. So after our Lord left this earth, He sent the Holy Spirit who through the Apostles caused the Jericho's and Ai's of Paganism to be overthrown and the greater part of the world to be evangelized. But after their occupancy of Canaan Israel's history was a sad one, being characterized by spiritual declination and departure from God. So it was with the professing church. Very quickly after the death of the Apostles heresy corrupted the Christian profession, and just as Israel of old grew tired of a theocracy and demanded a human head and king, like the nations which surrounded them, so the professing church became dissatisfied with the New Testament form of church government and submitted to the domination of a pope. And just as Israel's kings became more and more corrupt until God would bear with them no longer and sold His people into captivity, so after the setting up of the Papal See there followed the long period of the Dark Ages when Europe was subjected to a spiritual bondage and when the Word of God was bound in chains. Then, just as God raised up Ezra and Nehemiah to recover the living oracle and to lead out of their captivity a remnant of His people, so in the sixteenth century, A. D., God raised up Luther and honored contemporaries to bring about the great Reformation of Protestantism. Finally: just as after the days of Ezra and Hehemiah the Jews in Palestine witnessed a marked spiritual declination, ultimately lapsing into the ritualism of the Pharisees and the rationalism of the Sadducees from which God's elect were delivered only by the appearing of His own Son, so has history repeated itself. Since Reformation and the last of the Puritans, Christendom has moved swiftly in the direction of the predicted apostasy, and today we have reproduced the ancient Phariseeism in the rapid spread of Roman Catholicism, and the ancient Sadduceeism in the far-reaching effects of the infidelistic Higher Criticism: and as it was before, so it will be again—God's elect will be delivered only by the reappearing of our Lord and Savior Jesus Christ.

Thus we see how wonderfully and accurately the Old testament history runs parallel with and anticipated the history of the professing church in the New Testament dispensation. It has been truly said that "Coming events cast their shadows before them," and who but He who knows the end from the beginning and who upholds all things by the word of His power, could have caused the shadow of the Old Testament to have taken the shape they did, and thus give a true and comprehensive parabolic setting forth of that which has taken place thousands of years later!

But not only do the broad outlines of Old Testament history possess a typical meaning, everything in the Old Testament Scriptures has a spiritual value.

Every battle fought by the Israelites, every change in the administration of their government, every detail in their elaborate ceremonialism, and every personal biography narrated in the Bible, is designed for our instruction and edification. The Bible contains nothing that is superfluous. From beginning to end the Scriptures testify of Christ. Inanimate objects like the ark, which tells of security in Christ from the storms of Divine wrath; like the manna, which speaks of Him as the Bread of Life; like the brazen Serpent uplifted on the pole, of the Tabernacle, which presents Him as the meeting place of God and men—all foreshadowed the Redeemer. Living creatures like the Passover Lamb, the sacrificial bullocks, goats and rams, all pointed forward in general and in detail to the great Sacrifice for sins. Institutions like the Passover which prefigured His death; like the waving of the first-fruits, which forecast His resurrection; like the fast of Pentecost with its two loaves baken with leaven, telling of the uniting into one Body of the Jew and the Gentile; like the Burnt, the Meal and the Peace "sweet savor" offerings, which proclaimed the excellency of Christ's person in the esteem of God—all emblemized our blessed Savior. And, many of the leading personages of Old Testament biography gave a remarkable delineation of our Lord's character and earthly ministry.

Abel was a type of Christ. His name signifies vanity and emptiness which foreshadowed the Lord Jesus who "made Himself of no reputation," literally "emptied Himself" (Phil. 2:7), when He assumed the nature of man who is "like unto vanity" (Ps. 72:9). By calling, Abel, was a shepherd, and it was in his shepherd character he brought an offering to God, namely, the firstlings of his flock—speaking of the Good Shepherd who offered Himself to God. The offering which Abel brought to God is termed an "excellent" one (Heb. 11:4) and as such it pointed forward to the precious blood of Christ, the value of which cannot be estimated in silver and gold. Abel's offering was accepted by God, God "testifying" His approval of it; and, in like manner, God publicly witnessed to His acceptance of Christ's sacrifice when He raised Him from the Dead (Acts 2:32). Abel's offering still speaks to God—"by it he being dead, yet speaketh;" so, too, Christ's offering "speaks" to God (Heb. 12:24). Though guilty of no offense, Abel was hated by his brother and cruelly slain at his hand, foreshadowing the treatment which the Lord Jesus received at the hands of the Jews—His brethren according to the flesh.

Isaac was a type of Christ. he was the child of promise. His nativity was announced by an angel. He was supernaturally begotten. He was born at an appointed time. He was named by God (Gen.

1: 18-19). He was the "seed" to whom the promises were made and through whom they were secured. He became obedient unto death. He carried on his own shoulder the wood on which he was to be offered. He was securely fastened to the alter. He was presented as a sacrifice to God. He was offered on Mount Moriah—the same on which, two thousand years later, Jesus Christ was offered. And, it was on the "third day" that Abraham received him back "in a figure" from the dead (Heb. 11:19).

Joseph is a type of Christ. He was Jacob's well-beloved son. He readily responded to his father's will when asked to go on a mission to his brethren. While seeking his brethren he became a "wanderer in the field" (Gen. 37:15) —the "field" figuring the world (see Matt. 13:38). He found his brethren in Dothan which signifies the law—so the Lord Jesus found His brethren under the bondage of the law. His brethren mocked and refused to receive him. His brethren took counsel together against him that they might put him to death. Judah (Judas is the Greek form of the same word) advised his brethren to sell Joseph to the Ishmaelites. After he had been rejected by his brethren, Joseph was taken down into Egypt in order that he might become a Savior to the world. While in Egypt, Joseph was tempted, not without any compromise he put from him the evil solicitation. He was falsely accused and through no fault of his own was cast into prison. There he was the interpreter of dreams—the one who threw light on what was mysterious. In prison he became the savor of life to the butler, and the savor of death to the baker. After a period of humiliation and shame, he was exalted to the throne of Egypt. From that throne he administered bread to a hungering and perishing humanity. Subsequently Joseph became known to his brethren, and in fulfillment of what he had previously announced to them, they bowed down before him and owned his sovereignty.

Moses was a type of Christ. Moses became the adopted son of Pharaoh's daughter—so that legally he had a mother but no father, thus typifying our Lord's miraculous birth of a virgin. During infancy his life was endangered by the evil designs of the ... ruler. Like Christ's, his early life was spent in Egypt. Later, he renounced the position of royalty, refusing to be called the son of Pharaoh's daughter; and he who was rich, for the sake of his people, became poor. Before he commenced His life's work, a long period was spent in Midian in obscurity. Here he received a call and commission from God to go to deliver his brethren out of their terrible bondage. The credentials of his mission were seen in the miracles which he performed. Though despised and rejected by the rulers in Egypt, he, nevertheless, succeeded in delivering his own people. Subsequently, he became the leader and head of all Israel. In character he was the meekest man in all the earth. In all God's house he was faithful as a servant. In the wilderness he sent twelve men to spy out Canaan as our Lord sent out the twelve Apostles to preach the Gospel. He fasted for forty days. On the mount he was transfigured so that the skin of his face shone. He acted as God's prophet to the people, as as the people's intercessor before God. He was the only man mentioned in the Old Testament that was prophet, priest and king. He was the giver of a Law, the builder of a Tabernacle, and the organizer of a Priesthood. His last act was to "bless the people (Deut. 33:29), as our Lord's last act was to "bless" His disciples (Luke 24:50).

Samson was a type of Christ—see the Book on Judges. An angel announced his birth (13:3). From birth he was a Nazarite (13:5)—separated to God. Before he was born it was promised that he should be a savior to Israel (13:5). He was treated unkindly by his own nation (15:11-13). He was delivered up to the Gentiles by his own countrymen (15:12). He was mocked and cruelly treated by the Gentiles (16:19-21, 25) yet he was a mighty deliverer of Israel. His miracles were performed under the power of the Holy Spirit (14:19). He accomplished more in his death than he did in his life (16:30). He was imprisoned in the enemy's stronghold; the gates were barred, and a watch was set; yet, rising up at midnight, in the early hours of the morning—"a great while before day"—he burst the bars, broke open the gate, and issued forth triumphant—a remarkable type of our Lord's resurrection. He occupied the position of "judge," as our Lord will in the last great day.

David was a type of Christ. He was born in Bethlehem. He is described as "of a beautiful countenance and goodly to look upon." His name means "the beloved." By occupation he was a shepherd. During his shepherd life he entered into conflict with wild beasts. He slew Goliath—the opposer of God's people and a type of Satan. From the obscurity of shepherdhood he was exalted to Israel's throne. He was anointed as king before he was coronated. He was preeminently a man of prayer (see the Psalms) and is the only one in Scripture termed "The man after God's own heart." He was a man of sorrows and acquainted with grief, suffering chiefly from those of his own household. Repeated attempts were made upon his life by Israel's ruler. When his enemy (Saul) was in his power he refused to slay him, instead, he dealt with him in mercy and grace. He delivered Israel from all their enemies and vanquished all their foes.

Solomon was a type of Christ. He was Israel's king. His name signifies "Peaceable," and he foreshadows the millennial reign of the Lord Jesus when He shall rule as Prince of Peace. He was chosen and ordained of God before he was crowned. He rode upon another's mule, not as a warrior, but as the king of peace in lowly guise (1 Kings 1:33). Gentiles took part in the coronation of Solomon (1 Kings 1:38) typifying the universal homage which Christ shall receive during the millennium. The Cherethites and Pelethites were soldiers, so that Solomon was followed by an army at the time of his coronation (1 Kings 1:33; cp. Rev. 19:11). Solomon began his reign by showing mercy to and yet demanding righteousness from Adonijah (1 Kings 1:51)—such will be the leading characteristics of Christ's millennial government. Solomon was the builder of Israel's Temple (cp. Acts 15:16). At the dedication of the Temple, Solomon was the one who offered sacrifices unto the Lord: thus the king fulfilled the office of priest (1 Kings 8:63), which typifies the Lord Jesus who "shall be a Priest upon His throne" (Zech. 6:13). Solomon's "fame" went abroad far and wide and "all the earth sought to Solomon" (1 Kings 10:24). The queen of Sheba, representing the Gentiles, came up to Jerusalem to pay him homage (1 Kings 10) as all the nations will to Christ during the millennium (see Zech. 14:16). All Israel's land enjoyed rest and peace. The glory and magnificence of Solomon's reign has never been equaled before or since—"And the Lord magnified Solomon exceedingly in the sight of all Israel, and bestowed upon him such royal majesty as had not been on any king before him in Israel" (1 Chron. 29:25).

In the above types we have not sought to be exhaustive but suggestive by singling out only the leading lines in each typical picture. There are many other Old Testament characters who were types of Christ which we cannot now consider at length: Adam typified His Headship; Enoch His Ascension; Noah as the provider of a Refuge; Jacob as the one who served for a Wife; Aaron as the great High Priest; Joshua as the Captain of our salvation; Samuel as the Faithful Prophet; Elijah as the Miracle worker; Jeremiah as the despised and rejected Servant of God; Daniel as the Faithful Witness for God; Jonah as the One raised from the dead on the third day.

In closing this chapter let us apply the argument. Of the many typical persons in the Old Testament who prefigure the Lord Jesus Christ, the striking, the accurate, and the manifold lights, in which each exhibits Him is truly remarkable. No two of them represent Him from exactly the same viewpoint. Each one contributes a line or two to the picture, but all are needed to give a complete delineation. That an authentic history should supply a series of personages in different ages, whose characters, offices, and histories, should exactly correspond with those of Another who did not appear upon earth until centuries later, can only be accounted for on the supposition of Divine appointment. When we consider the utter dissimilarity of these typical persons to one another; when we note that they had little or nothing in common with each other; when we remember that each of them represents some peculiar feature in a composite Anti type; we discover that we have a literary phenomenon which is truly remarkable. Abel, Isaac, Joseph, Moses, Samson, David, Solomon (and all the others) are each deficient when viewed separately; but when looked at in conjunction they form an harmonious whole, and give us a complete representation of our Lord's miraculous birth, His peerless character, His life's mission, His sacrificial death, His triumphant resurrection, His ascension to heaven, and His millennial reign. Who could have invented such character? How remarkable that the earliest history in the world, extending from the creation and reaching to the last of the prophets—written by various hands through a period of fifteen centuries—should from start to finish concentrate in a single point, and that point the person and work of the blessed Redeemer! Verily, such a Book must have been written by God—no other conclusion is possible. Beneath the historical we discern the spiritual: behind the incidental we behold the typical: underneath the human biographies we see the form of Christ, and in these things we discover on every page of the Old Testament the "watermark" of heaven.

CHAPTER SEVEN
THE WONDERFUL UNITY OF THE BIBLE ATTESTS ITS DIVINE AUTHORSHIP

The manner in which the Bible has been produced argues against its unity. The Bible was penned on two continents, written in three languages, and its composition and compilation extended through the slow progress of sixteen centuries. The various parts of the Bible were written at different times and under the most varying circumstances. Parts of it were written in tents, deserts, cities, palaces and dungeons; in times of imminent danger and in seasons of ecstatic joy. Among its writers were judges, kings, priests, prophets, patriarchs, prime ministers, herdsmen, scribes, soldiers, physicians and fishermen. Yet despite these varying circumstances, conditions and workmen, the Bible is one Book, behind its many parts there is an unmistakable organic unity. It contains one system of doctrine, one code of ethics, one plan of salvation and one rule of faith.

Now if forty different men were selected today from such varying stations and callings of life as to include clerks, rulers, politicians, judges, clergy, doctors, farm laborers and fishermen, and each was asked to contribute a chapter for some book on theology or church government, when their several contributions were collected and bound together, would there be any unity about them, could that book truly be said to be one book; or would not their different productions vary so much in literary value, diction and matter as to be merely a heterogeneous mass, a miscellaneous collection? Yet we do not find this to be the case in connection with God's Book. Although the Bible is a volume of sixty-six Books, written by forty different men, treating of such a large variety of themes as to cover nearly the whole range of human inquiry, we find it is one Book, the Book (not the books), the Bible.

Further; if we were to select specimens of literature from the third, fifth, tenth, fifteenth and twentieth centuries of the Christian era and were to bind them together, what unity and harmony should we find in such a collection? Human writers reflect the spirit of their own day and generation and the compositions of men living amid widely differing influences and separated by centuries of time have little or nothing in common with each other. Yet although the earliest portions of the Sacred Canon date back to at least the fifteenth century, B. C., while the writings of John were not completed till the close of the first century, A. D., nevertheless, we find a perfect harmony throughout the Scriptures from the first verse in Genesis to the last verse in Revelation. The great ethical and spiritual lessons presented in the Bible, by whoever taught, agree.

The more one really studies the Bible the more one is convinced that behind the many human mouths there is One overruling, controlling Mind. Imagine forty persons of different nationalities, possessing various degrees of musical culture visiting the organ of some cathedral and at long intervals of time, and without any collusion whatever, striking sixty-six different notes, which when combined yielded the theme of the grandest oratorio ever heard: would it not show that behind these forty different men there was one presiding mind, one great Tone master? As we listen to some great orchestra, with an immense variety of instruments playing their different parts, but producing melody and harmony, we realize that at the back of these many musicians there is the personality and genius of the composer. And when we enter the halls of the Divine Academy and listen to the heavenly choirs singing the Song of Redemption, all in perfect accord and unison, we know that it is God Himself who has written the music and put this song into their mouths.

We now submit two illustrations which demonstrate the unity of the Holy Scriptures. Certain grand conceptions run through the entire Bible like a cord on which are strung so many precious pearls. First and foremost among them is the Divine Plan of Redemption. Just as the scarlet thread runs through all the cordage of the British Navy, so a crimson aura surrounds every page of God's Word.

In the Scriptures the Plan of Redemption is central and fundamental. In Genesis we have recorded the Creation and Fall of man to show that he has the capacity for and is in need of redemption. Next we find the Promise of the Redeemer, for man requires to have before him the hope and expectation of a Savior. Then follows an elaborate system of sacrifices and offerings and these represent pictorially the nature of redemption and the condition under which salvation is realized. At the commencement of the New Testament we have the four Gospels and they set forth the Basis of Redemption, namely, the Incarnation, Life, Death, Resurrection and Ascension of the Redeemer. Next comes the Book of the Acts which illustrates again and again the Power of Redemption, showing that it is adequate to work its great results in the salvation of both Jew and Gentile. Finally, in the Revelation, we are shown the ultimate triumphs of redemption, the Goal of Salvation—the redeemed dwelling with God in perfect union and communion. Thus we see that though a large number of human media were employed in the writing of the Bible, yet their productions are not independent of each other, but are complementary and supplementary parts of one great whole; that one sublime truth is common to them all, namely, man's need of redemption and God's provision of a Redeemer. And the only explanation of this fact is, that "All Scripture is given by inspiration of God."

Secondly; among all the many personalities presented in the Bible, we find that one stands out above all others, not merely prominent but preeminent. Just as in the scene unveiled in the fifth chapter of the Revelation we find the Lamb in the center of the heavenly throngs, so we find that in the Scriptures also, the Lord Jesus Christ is accorded the place which alone befits His unique Person. Considered from one standpoint the Scriptures are really the biography of the Son of God.

In the Old Testament we have the Promise of our Lord's Incarnation and Mediatorial work. In the Gospels we have the Proclamation of His Mission and the Proofs of His Messianic claims and authority. In the Acts we have a demonstration of His saving Power and the execution of His missionary Program. In the Epistles we find an exposition and amplification of His Precepts for the education of His People. While in the Apocalypse we behold the unveiling or Presentation of His Person and the Preparation of the earth for His Presence. The Bible is therefore seen to be peculiarly the Book of Jesus Christ. Christ not only testified to the Scriptures but each section of the Scriptures testify of Him. Every page of the Holy Book has stamped upon it His photograph and every chapter bears His autograph. He is its one great theme, and the only explanation of this fact is that, the Holy Spirit superintended the work of each and every writer of the Scriptures.

The unity of the Scriptures is further to be seen on the fact that they are entirely free from any real contradictions. Though different writers often described the same incidents—as for example the four evangelists recording the facts relating to our Lord's ministry and redemptive work—and though there is considerable variety in the narrations of these, yet there are no real discrepancies. The harmony existing between them does not appear on the surface, but, often, is only discovered by protracted study, though it is there nevertheless. Moreover, there is perfect agreement of doctrine between all the writers in the Bible. The teaching of the prophets and the teaching of the Apostles on the great truths of God's righteousness, the demands of His holiness, the utter ruin of man, the exceeding sinfulness of sin, and the way of salvation, is entirely harmonious. This might appear a thing easily affected. But those who are acquainted with human nature, and have read widely the writings of men, will acknowledge that nothing but the inspiration of the writers can explain this fact. Nowhere can we find two uninspired writers, however similar they may have been in their religious sentiments, who agree in all points of doctrine. Nay, entire consistency of sentiment is not to be found even in the writings of the same author at different periods. In his later years Spurgeon's statement of some doctrines was much more modified than the utterances of his earlier days. Increasing knowledge causes men to change their views upon many subjects. But among the writers of Scripture there is the most perfect harmony, because they obtained their knowledge of truth and duty not by the efforts of study, but from inspiration by the Holy Spirit of God.

When therefore we find that in the productions of forty different men there is perfect accord and concord, unison and unity, harmony in all their teachings, and the same conceptions pervading all their writings, the conclusion is irresistible that behind their minds, and guiding their hands, there was the master-mind of God Himself. Does not the unity of the Bible illustrate the Divine Inspiration of the Bible and demonstrate the truth of its own assertion that "God (who) at sundry times and in divers manners spoke in time past unto the fathers by the prophets" (Heb. 1:1)?

CHAPTER EIGHT
THE MARVELOUS INFLUENCE OF THE BIBLE DECLARES ITS SUPER-HUMAN CHARACTER

The influence of the Bible is world-wide. Its mighty power has affected every department of human activity. The contents of the Scriptures have supplied themes for the greatest poets, artists and musicians which the world has yet produced, and have been the mightiest factor of all in shaping the moral progress of the race. Let us consider a few examples of the Bible's influence as displayed in the various realms of human enterprise.

Take away such sublime oratorios as "Elijah" and "The Messiah," and you have taken out of the realm of music something which can never be duplicated; destroy the countless hymns which have drawn their inspiration from the Scriptures and you have left us little else worth singing.

Eliminate from the compositions of Tennyson, Wordsworth and Carlisle every reference to the moral and spiritual truths taught in God's Word and you have stripped them of their beauty and robbed them of their fragrance. Take down from off the walls of our best Art Galleries those pictures which portray scenes and incidents in the history of Israel and the life of our Lord and you have removed the richest gems from the crown of human genius. Remove from our statute books every law which is founded upon the ethical conceptions of the Bible and you have annihilated the greatest factor in modern civilization. Rob our libraries of every book which is devoted to the work of elaborating and disseminating the precepts and concepts of Holy Writ and you have taken from us that which cannot be valued in dollars and cents.

The Bible has done more for the emancipation and civilization of the heathen than all the forces which the human arm can wield, put together. Someone has said, "Draw a line around the nations which have the Bible and you will then have divided between barbarism and civilization, between thrift and poverty, between selfishness and charity, between oppression and freedom, between life and the shadow of death." Even Darwin had to concede the miraculous element in the triumphs of the missionaries of the cross.

Here are two or three men who land on a savage island. Its inhabitants possess no literature and have no written language. They regard the white man as their enemy and have no desire to be shown "the error of their ways." They are cannibals by instinct and little better than the brute beasts in their habits of life. The missionaries who have entered their midst have no money with which to buy their friendship, no army to compel their obedience and no merchandise to stir their avarice. Their only weapon is "the Sword of the Spirit," their only capital "the unsearchable riches of Christ," their only offer the invitation of the Gospel. Yet somehow they succeed, and without the shedding of any blood gain the victory. In a few short years naked savagery is changed to the garb of civilization, lust is transformed into purity, cruelty is now kindness, avarice has become unselfishness, and where before vindictiveness existed there is now to be seen meekness and the spirit of loving self-sacrifice. And this has been accomplished by the Bible! This miracle is still being repeated in every part of the earth! What other book, or library of books, could work such a result? Is it not evident to all that the Book which does exert such a unique and unrivaled influence must be vitalized by the life of God Himself?

This wonderful characteristic, namely the unique influence of the Bible, is rendered the more remarkable when we take into account the antiquity of the Scriptures! The last Books which were added to the Sacred Canon are now more than eighteen hundred years old, yet the workings of the Bible are as mighty in their effects today as they were in the first century of the Christian era.

The power of man's books soon wane and disappear. With but few exceptions the productions of the human intellect enjoy a brief existence. As a general rule the writings of man within fifty years of their first public appearance lie untouched on the top shelves of our libraries. Man's writings are like himself—dying creatures. Man comes onto the age of this world, plays his part in the drama of life, influences the audience while he is acting, but is forgotten as soon as the curtain falls upon his brief career; so it is with his writings. While they are fresh and new they amuse, interest or

The Divine Inspiration of the Bible

instruct as the wise may be, and then die a natural death. Even the few exceptions to this rule only exert a very limited influence, their power is circumscribed; they are unread by the great majority, yea, are unknown to the biggest portion of our race. But how different with God's Book! The written Word, like the Living Word, is "The same yesterday, and today, and forever," and unlike any other book it has made its way into all countries and speaks with equal clearness, directness and force to all men in their mother tongue. The Bible never becomes antiquated, its vitality never diminishes and its influence is more irresistible and universal today than it was two thousand years ago. Such facts as these declare with no uncertain voice that the Bible is endued with the same Divine life and energy as its Author, for in no other way can we account for its marvelous influence through the centuries and its mighty power upon the world.

Arthur W. Pink

CHAPTER NINE
THE MIRACULOUS POWER OF THE BIBLE SHOWS FORTH THAT ITS INSPIRER IS THE ALMIGHTY

I. The Power of God's Word to Convict Men of Sin.

In Hebrews 4:12 we have a Scripture which draws attention to this peculiar characteristic of the Bible—"For the Word of God is quick, and powerful, and sharper than any two edged sword, piercing even to the dividing asunder of soul and spirit, and of the joints and marrow, and is a discerner of the thoughts and intents of the heart." The writings of men may sometimes stir the emotions, search the conscience, and influence the human will, but in a manner and degree possessed by no other book the Bible convicts men of their guilt and lost estate. The Word of God is the Divine mirror, for in it man reads the secrets of his own guilty soul and sees the vileness of his own evil nature. In a way absolutely peculiar to themselves, the Scriptures discern the thoughts and intents of the heart and reveal to men the fact that they are lost sinners and in the presence of a Holy God.

Some thirty years ago there resided in one of the Temples of Thibet a Buddhist priest who had conversed with no Christian missionary, had heard nothing about the cross of Christ, and had never seen a copy of the Word of God. One day while searching for something in the temple, he came across a transcription of Matthew's Gospel, which years before had been left there by a native who had received it from some traveling missionary. His curiosity aroused, the Buddhist priest commenced to read it, but when he reached the eighth verse in the fifth chapter he paused and pondered over it: "Blessed are the pure in heart: for they shall see God." Although he knew nothing about the righteousness of his Maker, although he was quite ignorant concerning the demands of God's holiness, yet he was there and then convicted of his sins, and a work of Divine grace commenced in his soul. Month after month went by and each day he said to himself, "I shall never see God, for I am impure in heart." Slowly but surely the work of the Holy Spirit deepened within him until he saw himself as a lost sinner; vile, guilty, and undone.

After continuing for more than a year in this miserable condition the priest one day heard that a "foreign devil" was visiting a town nearby and selling books which spoke about God. The same night the Buddhist priest fled from the temple and journeyed to the town where the missionary was residing. On reaching his destination he sought out the missionary and at once said to him, "Is it true that only those who are pure in heart will see God?" "Yes," replied the missionary, "but the same Book which tells you that, also tells you how you may obtain a pure heart," and then he talked to him about our Lord's atoning work and how that "the blood of Jesus Christ His Son cleanseth us from all sin." Quickly the light of God flooded the soul of the Buddhist priest and he found the peace which "passeth all understanding." Now what other book in the world outside of the Bible, contains a sentence or even a chapter which, without the aid of any human commentator, is capable of convincing and convicting a heathen that he is a lost sinner? Does not the fact of the miraculous power of the Bible, which has been illustrated by thousands of fully authenticated cases similar to the above, declare that the Scriptures are the inspired Word of God, vested with the same might as their Omnipotent Author?

II. The Power of God's Word to Deliver Men From Sin.

A single incident which was brought before the notice of the writer must suffice to illustrate the above mentioned truth.

Some forty years ago a Christian gentleman stood upon the quay of the Liverpool docks distributing tracts to the sailors. In the course of his work he handed one to a man who was just embarking on a voyage to China, and with an oath the sailor took it, crumpled it up and thrust it into his pocket. Some three weeks after, this sailor was down in his cabin and needing a "spell" with which to light his pipe felt in his pocket for the necessary paper and drew out the little tract which he had received in Liverpool. On recognizing it he uttered a terrible oath and tore the paper in pieces. One small fragment adhered to his tarry hand and glancing at it he saw these words, "Prepare to meet thy God." When relating the incident to the writer he said, "It was at that moment as though a sword had pierced my heart." "Prepare to meet thy God" rang again and again in his ears, and with a strickened conscience he was tormented about his lost condition. Presently he retired for the night, but sleep he could not. In desperation he got up and dressed and went above and paced the deck. Hour after hour he walked up and down, but try as he might he could not dismiss from his mind the words, "Prepare to meet thy God." For years this man had been a helpless slave in the grip of strong drink and knowing his weakness he said: "How can I prepare to meet God, when I am so powerless to overcome my besetting sin?" Finally, he got down upon his knees and cried: "O God, have mercy on me, save me from my sins, deliver me from the power of drink and help me prepare for the meeting with Thee." More than thirty-five years after, this converted sailor told the writer that from the night he had read that quotation from God's Word, had prayed that prayer, and had accepted Christ as his Savior from sin, he had never tasted a single drop of intoxicating liquor and had never once had a desire to craving for strong drink. How marvelous is the power of God's Word to deliver men from sin! Truly, as Dr. Torrey has well said, "A Book which will lift men up to God must have come down from God."

III. The Power of God's Word Over the Human Affections.

In thousands of instances men and women have been stretched upon the "rack," torn limb from limb, thrown to the wild beasts, and have been burned at the stake rather than abandon the Bible and promise never again to read its sacred pages. For what other book would men and women suffer and die?

More than two hundred years ago when a copy of the Bible was much more expensive than it is in these days, a peasant who lived in the County of Cork, Ireland, heard that a gentleman in his neighborhood had a copy of the New testament in the Irish language. Accordingly he visited this man and asked to be allowed to see it, and after looking at it with great interest begged to be allowed to copy it. Knowing how poor the peasant was the gentleman asked him where he would get his paper and ink from? "I will buy them," was the reply. "And where will you find a place to write?" "If your honor will allow me the use of your hall, I'll come after my day's work is over and copy a little at a time in the evenings." The gentleman was so moved at this man's intense

The Divine Inspiration of the Bible

love of the Bible that he gave him the use of his hall and light and provided him with paper and ink as well. True to his purpose and promise, the peasant labored night after night until he had written out a complete copy of the New Testament. Afterwards a printed copy was given to him, and the written Testament is preserved by the British and Foreign Bible Society. Again, we ask, what other book in the world could obtain such a hold upon the affections and win such love and reverence, and produce such self-sacrificing toil?

Arthur W. Pink

CHAPTER TEN
THE COMPLETENESS OF THE BIBLE DEMONSTRATES ITS DIVINE PERFECTION

The antiquity of the Scriptures argues against their completeness. The compilation of the Bible was completed more than eighteen centuries ago, while the greater part of the world was yet uncivilized. Since John added the capstone to the Temple of God's Truth there have been many wonderful discoveries and inventions, yet there have been no additions whatever to the moral and spiritual truths contained in the Bible. Today, we know no more about the origin of life, the nature of the soul, the problem of suffering or the future destiny of man than did those who had the Bible eighteen hundred years ago. Through the centuries of the Christian era, man has succeeded in learning many of the secrets of nature and has harnessed her forces to his service, but in the actual revelation of supernatural truth nothing new has been discovered. Human writers cannot supplement the Divine records for they are complete, entire, "wanting nothing."

The Bible needs no addendum. There is more than sufficient in God's Word to meet the temporal and spiritual needs of all mankind. Though written two thousand years ago, the Bible is still "up-to-date," and answers every vital question which concerns the soul of man in our day. The Book of Job was written three thousand years before Columbus discovered America, yet it is as fresh to the heart of man now as though it had only been published ten years ago. The majority of the Psalms were written two thousand five hundred years before President Wilson was born, yet in our day and generation they are perfectly new and fresh to the human soul. Such facts as these can only be explained on the hypothesis that the Eternal God is the Author of the Bible.

The adaptation of the Scriptures is another illustration of their wonderful completeness. To young or old, feeble or vigorous, ignorant or cultured, joyful or sorrowful, perplexed or enlightened,

The Divine Inspiration of the Bible

Orientalist or Ocidentalist, saint or sinner, the Bible is a source of blessing, will minister to every need, and is able to supply every variety of want. And the Bible is the only Book in the world of which this can be predicted. The writings of Plato may be a source of interest and instruction to the philosophic mind, but they are unsuitable for placing in the hands of a child. Not so with the Bible: the youngest may profit from a perusal of the Sacred Page. The writings of Jerome or Twain may please, for an hour, the man of humor, but they will bring no balm to the sore heart and will speak no words of comfort and consolation to those passing through the waters of bereavement. How different with the Scriptures—never has a heavy heart turned in vain to God's Word for peace! The writings of Shakespeare, Goethe, and Schiller may be of profit to the Western mind, but they convey little of value to the Easterner. Not so with God's Word; it may be translated into any language and will speak with equal clearness, directness and power to all men in their mother tongue.

To quote Dr. Burrell: "In every heart, down below all other wants and aspirations, there is a profound longing to know the way of spiritual life. The world is crying, "What shall I do to be saved?" Of all books the Bible is the only one that answers that universal cry. There are other books which set forth morality with more or less correctness; but there is none other that suggests a blotting out of the record of the mislived past or an escape from the penalty of the broken law. There are other books that have poetry; but there is none that sings the song of salvation or gives a troubled soul the peace that floweth like a river. There are other books that have eloquence; but there is no other that enables us to behold God Himself with outstretched hands pleading with men to turn and live. There are other books that have science; but there is none other that can give the soul a definite assurance of the future life, so that it can say, "I know whom I have believed, and am persuaded that He is able to keep that which I have committed unto Him against that day."

Though other books contain valuable truths, they also have an admixture of error; other books contain part of the truth, the Bible alone contains all the truth. Nowhere in the writings of human genius can a single moral or spiritual truth be found, which is not contained in substance in the Bible. Examine the writings of the ancients; ransack the libraries of Egypt, Assyria, Persia,

India, Greece, and Rome; search the contents of the Koran, the Zend-Avesta, or the Bagavad-Gita; gather together the most exalted spiritual thoughts and the sublimest moral conceptions contained in them and you will find that each and all are duplicated in the Bible! Dr. Torrey has said, "If every book but the Bible were destroyed not a single spiritual truth would be lost." In the small compass of God's Word there is stored more wisdom which will endure the test of eternity than the sum total of thinking done by man since his creation. Of all the books in the world, the Bible alone can truly be said to be complete, and this characteristic of the Scriptures is another of the many lines of demonstration which witnesses to the Divine inspiration of the Bible.

CHAPTER ELEVEN
THE INDESTRUCTIBILITY OF THE BIBLE IS A PROOF THAT ITS AUTHOR IS DIVINE

The survival of the Bible through the ages is very difficult to explain if it is not in truth the Word of God. Books are like men—dying creatures. A very small percentage of books survive more than twenty years, a yet smaller percentage last a hundred years and only a very insignificant fraction represent those which have lived a thousand years. Amid the wreck and ruin of ancient literature the Holy Scriptures stand out like the last survivor of an otherwise extinct race, and the very fact of the Bible's continued existence is an indication that like its Author it is indestructible.

When we bear in mind the fact that the Bible has been the special object of never ending persecution the wonder of the Bible's survival is changed into a miracle. Not only has the Bible been the most intensely loved Book in all the world, but it has also been the most bitterly hated. Not only has the Bible received more veneration and adoration than any other book, but it has also been the object of more persecution and opposition. For two thousand years man's hatred of the Bible has been persistent, determined, relentless and murderous. Every possible effort has been made to undermine faith in the inspiration and authority of the Bible and innumerable enterprises have been undertaken with the determination to consign it to oblivion. Imperial edicts have been issued to the effect that every known copy of the Bible should be destroyed, and when this measure failed to exterminate and annihilate God's Word then commands were given that every person found with a copy of the Scriptures in his possession should be put to death. The very fact that the Bible has been so singled out for such relentless persecution causes us to wonder at such a unique phenomenon.

Although the Bible is the best Book in the world yet is has produced more enmity and opposition than has the combined contents of all our libraries. Why should this be? Clearly because the Scriptures convict men of their guilt and condemn them for their sins! Political and ecclesiastical powers have united in the attempt to put the Bible out of existence, yet their concentrated efforts have utterly failed. After all the persecution which has assailed the Bible, it is, humanly speaking, a wonder that there is any Bible left at all. Every engine of destruction which human philosophy, science, force, and hatred could bring against a book has been brought against the Bible, yet it stands unshaken and unharmed today. When we remember that no army has defended the Bible and no king has ever ordered its enemies to be extirpated, our wonderment increases. At times nearly all the wise and great of the earth have been pitted together against the Bible, while only a few despised ones have honored and revered it. The cities of the ancients were lighted with bonfires made of Bibles, and for centuries only those in hiding dare read it. How then, can we account for the survival of the Bible in the face of such bitter persecution? The only solution is to be found in the promise of God. "Heaven and earth shall pass away, but My words shall not pass away."

The story of the Bible's persecution is an arresting one. During the first three centuries of the Christian era the Roman Emperors sought to destroy God's Word. One of them, named Diocletian, believed that he had succeeded. He had slain so many Christians and destroyed so many Bibles, that when the lovers of the Bible remained quiet for a season and kept in hiding, he imagined that he had made an end of the Scriptures. So elated was he at this achievement, he ordered a medal to be struck inscribed with the words, "The Christian religion is destroyed and the worship of the gods restored." One wonders what that emperor would think if he returned to this earth today and found that more had been written about the Bible than about any other thousand books put together, and that the Bible which enshrines the Christian faith is now translated into more than four hundred languages and is being sent out to every part of the earth!

Centuries after the persecution by the Roman Emperors, when the Roman Catholic Church obtained command of the city of Rome, the Pope and his priests took up the old quarrel against the Bible. The Holy Scriptures were taken away from the people, copies of the Bible were forbidden to be purchased and all who were found with a copy of God's Word in their possession were tortured and killed. For centuries the Roman Catholic Church bitterly persecuted the Bible and it was not until the time of the Reformation at the close of the sixteenth century that the Word of God was again given to the masses in their own tongue.

Even in our day the persecution of the Bible still continues, though the method of attack is changed. Much of our modern scholarship is engaged in the work of seeking to destroy faith in the Divine inspiration and authority of the Bible. In many of our seminaries the rising generation of the clergy are taught that Genesis is a book of myths, that much of the teaching of the Pentateuch is immoral, that the historical records of the Old Testament are unreliable and that the whole Bible is man's creation rather than God's revelation. And so the attack on the Bible is being perpetuated.

Now suppose there was a man who had lived upon this earth for eighteen hundred years, that this man had oftentimes been thrown into the sea and yet could not be drowned; that he had frequently been cast before wild beasts who were unable to devour him; that he had many times been made to drink deadly poisons which never did him any harm; that he had often been bound in iron chains and locked in prison dungeons, yet he had always been able to throw off the chains and escape from his captivity; that he had repeatedly been hanged, till his enemies thought him dead, yet when his body was cut down he sprang to his feet and walked away as though nothing had happened; that hundreds of times he had been burned at the stake, till there seemed to be nothing left of him, yet as soon as the fires were out he leaped up from the ashes as well and as vigorous as ever—but we need not expand this idea any further; such a man would be super-human, a miracle of miracles. Yet this is exactly how we should regard the Bible! This is practically the way in which the Bible has been treated. It has been burned, drowned, chained, put in prison, and torn to pieces, yet never destroyed!

No other book has provoked such fierce opposition as the Bible, and its preservation is perhaps the most startling miracle connected with it. But two thousand five hundred years ago God declared, "The grass withereth, the flower fadeth, but the Word of our God shall abide forever." Just as the three Hebrews passed safely through the fiery furnace of Nebuchadnezzar unharmed and unscorched, so the Bible has emerged from the furnace of satanic hatred and assault without even the smell of fire upon it! Just as an earthly parent treasures and lays by the letters received from his child, so our Heavenly Father has protected and preserved the Epistles of love written to His children.

CHAPTER TWELVE
INWARD CONFIRMATION OF THE VERACITY OF THE SCRIPTURES

We are living in a day when confidence is lacking; when skepticism and agnosticism are becoming more and more prevalent; and when doubt and uncertainty are made the badges of culture and wisdom. Everywhere men are demanding proof. Hypotheses and speculations fail to satisfy: the heart cannot rest content until it is able to say, "I know." The demand of the human mind is for definite knowledge and positive assurance. And God has condescended to meet this need.

One thing which distinguishes Christianity from all human systems is that it deals with absolute certainties. Christians are people who know. And well it is that they do. The issues concerning life and death are so stupendous, the stake involved in the salvation of the soul is so immense, that we cannot afford to be uncertain here. None but a fool would attempt to cross a frozen river until he was sure that the ice was strong enough to bear him. Dare we then face the river of death with nothing but a vague and uncertain hope to rest upon? Personal assurance is the crying need of the hour. There can be no peace and joy until this is attained. A parent who is in suspense concerning the safety of his child, is in agony of soul. A criminal who lies in the condemned cell hoping for a reprieve, is in mental torment until his pardon arrives. And a professed Christian who knows not whether he shall ultimately land in Heaven or Hell, is a pitiable object.

But we say again, real Christians are people who know. They know that their Redeemer liveth (John 19:25). They know that they have passed from death unto life (1 John 3:14). They know that all things work together for good (Rom. 8:28). They know that if their earthly house of this tabernacle were dissolved, they have a building of God, a house not made with hands, eternal in the heavens (2 Cor. 5:1). They know that one day they shall see Christ face to face and be made like Him (1 John 3:2). In the meantime they know whom they have believed, and are persuaded that He is able to keep that which they have committed unto Him against that day (2 Tim. 1:12). If it be asked, How do they know, the answer is, they have proven for themselves the trustworthiness of God's Word which affirms these things.

The force of this present argument will appeal to none save those who have an experimental acquaintance with it. In addition to all the external proofs that we have for the Divine Inspiration of the Scriptures, the believer has a source of evidence to which no unbeliever has access. In his own experience the Christian finds a personal confirmation of the teachings of God's Word. To the man whose life which, judged by the standards of the world, appears morally upright, the statement that "the heart is deceitful above all things and desperately wicked" seems to be the gloomy view of a pessimist, or a description which has no general application. But the believer has found that "the entrance of Thy words giveth light" (Ps. 119:30), and in the light of God's Word and beneath the illuminating power of God's Spirit who indwells him, he has discovered there is within him a sink of iniquity. To natural wisdom, which is fond of philosophizing about the freedom of the human will, the declaration of Christ that "No man can come to Me, except the Father which hath sent Me, draw him" (John 6:44) seems a hard saying; but, to the one who has been taught by the Holy Spirit something of the binding power of sin, such a declaration has been verified in his own experience. To the one who has done his best to live up to the light which he had, and has sought to develop an honest and amiable character, such a statement as, "All our righteousnesses are as filthy rags," seems unduly harsh and severe; but to the man who has received "an unction from the Holy One," his very best works appear to him sordid and sinful; and such they are. The Apostle's confession that "in me (that is, in my flesh,) dwelleth no good thing" (Rom. 7:18) which once appeared absurd to him, the believer now acknowledges to be his own condition. The description of the Christian which is found in Romans...is something which none but a regenerate person can understand. The things there mentioned as belonging to the same man at the same time, seem foolish to the wise of this world; but the believer realizes completely the truth of it in his own life.

The promises of God can be tested: their trustworthiness is capable of verification. In the Gospel Christ promises to give rest to all those who are weary and heavy laden that come unto Him. He declares that He came to seek and to save that which was lost. He affirms that "whosoever drinketh of the Water that I shall give him shall never thirst." In short, the Gospel presents the Lord Jesus Christ as a Savior. His claim to save can be put to the proof. Yea, it has been, and that by a multitude of individuals that no man can number. Many of these are living on earth today. Every individual who has read in the Scriptures the invitations that are addressed to sinners, and has personally appropriated them to himself, can say n the words of the well-known hymn:—

> "I came to Jesus as I was.
> Weary and worn and sad;
> I found in Him a resting place
> And He has made me glad."

Should these pages be read by a skeptic who, despite his present unbelief, has a sincere and earnest desire to know the truth, he, too may put God's Word to the test and share the experience described above. It is written, "Believe on the Lord Jesus Christ and thou shalt be saved,"—believe, my reader, and thou, too, shalt be saved.

"We speak that we do know, and testify that we have seen" (John 3:11). The Bible testifies to the fact that "all have sinned and come short of the glory of God," and our own conscience confirms it. The Bible declares that it is "not by works of righteousness which we have down, but according to His mercy" God saves us; and the Christian has proven that he was unable to do anything to win God's esteem: but, having cried the prayer of the Publican, he has gone down to his house justified. The Bible teaches that "if any man be in Christ, he is a new creature: old things are passed away; behold, all things are become new;" and the believer has found that the things he once hated he now loves, and that the things he hitherto counted gain he now regards as dross. The Bible witnesses to the fact that we "are kept by the power of God through faith," and the believer has proven that though the world, the flesh, and the devil are arrayed against him, yet the grace of God is sufficient for all his need. Ask the Christian, then, why he believes that the Bible is the Word of God, and he will tell you, Because it has done for me what it professes to do (save); because

I have tested its promises for myself; because I find its teachings verified in my own experiences.

To the unregenerate the Bible is practically a sealed Book. Even the cultured and educated are unable to understand its teachings: parts of it appear plain and simple, but much of it is dark and mysterious. This is exactly what the Bible declares—"The natural man receiveth not the things of the Spirit of God: for they are foolishness unto him: neither can he know them, because they are spiritually discerned" (1 Cor. 2:14). But to the man of God it is otherwise: "He that believeth on the Son of God hath the witness in himself" (1 John 5:10). As the Lord Jesus declared, "If any man will do His will, he shall know of the doctrine" (John 7:17). While the infidel stumbles in darkness, even in the midst of light, the believer discovers the evidence of its truth in himself with the clearness of a sunbeam. "For God, who commanded the light to shine out of darkness, hath shined in our hearts, to give the light of the knowledge of the glory of God in the face of Jesus Christ" (2 Cor. 4:6).

CHAPTER THIRTEEN
VERBAL INSPIRATION

Not only does the Bible claim to be a Divine revelation but it also asserts that its original manuscripts were written "not in the words which man's wisdom teacheth, but which the Holy Spirit teacheth" (1 Cor. 2:13). The Bible nowhere claims to have been written by inspired men—as a matter of fact some of them were very defective characters—Balaam for example—but it insists that the words they uttered and recorded were God's words. Inspiration has not to do with the minds of the writers (for many of them understood not what they wrote (1 Pet. 1:10-11), but with the writings themselves. "All Scripture is given by inspiration of God," and "Scripture" means "the writings." Faith has to do with God's Word and not with the men who wrote it—these are all dead long since, but their writings remain.

A writing that is inspired by God self-evidently implies, in the very expression, that the words are the words of God. To say that the inspiration of the Scriptures applies to their concepts and not to their words; to declare that one part of Scripture is written with one kind or degree of inspiration and another part with another kind or degree, is not only destitute of any foundation or support in the Scriptures themselves, but is repudiated by every statement in the Bible which bears upon the subject now under consideration. To say that the Bible is not the Word of God but merely contains the Word of God is the figment of an ill-employed ingenuity and an unholy attempt to depreciate and invalidate the supreme authority of the Oracles of God. All the attempts which have been made to explain the rationale of inspiration have done nothing toward simplifying the subject, rather have they tended to mystify. It is no easier to conceive how ideas without words could be imparted, than that Divinely revealed truths should be communicated by words. Instead of being diminished the difficulty is increased. It was as logical to talk of a sum without figures or a tune without notes, as of a Divine revelation and communication without words. Instead of speculation our duty is to receive and believe what the Scriptures say of themselves.

What the Bible teaches about its own inspiration is a matter purely of Divine testimony, and our business is simply to receive the testimony and not to speculate about or seek to pry into its modus operandi. Inspiration is as much a matter of Divine revelation as is justification by faith. Both stand equally on the authority of the Scriptures themselves, which must be the final court of appeal on this subject as on every question of revealed truth.

The teaching of the Bible concerning the inspiration of the Scriptures is clear and simple, and uniform throughout. Its writers were conscious that their utterances were a message from God in the highest meaning of the word. "And the Lord said unto him (Moses), Who hath made man's mouth? or who maketh the dumb, or deaf, or the seeing, or the blind? Have not I the Lord? Now therefore go, and I will be with thy mouth, and teach thee what thou shalt say" (Exod. 4:11-12). "The Spirit of the Lord spoke by me, and His word was in my tongue" (2 Sam. 23:2). "Then the Lord put forth His hand, and touched my mouth. and the Lord said unto me, Behold, I have put My words in thy mouth" (Jer. 1:9). The above are only a sample of scores of similar passages which might be sighted.

What is predicted of the Scriptures themselves, demonstrates that they are entirely and absolutely the Word of God. "The law of the Lord is perfect, converting the soul" (Ps. 19:7)—this altogether excludes any place in the Bible for human infirmities and imperfections. "Thy Word is very pure" (Ps. 119:140), which cannot mean less than that the Holy Spirit so superintended the composition of the Bible and so "moved" its writers that all error has been excluded. "Thy Word is true from the beginning" (Ps. 119:160)—how this anticipated the assaults of the higher critics on the Book of Genesis, particularly on its opening chapters!

The teaching of the New Testament agrees with what we have quoted from the Old. "Take ye no thought how or what thing ye shall answer, or what ye shall say: for the Holy Spirit shall teach you in the same hour what ye ought to say" (Luke 12:11-12),—the disciples were the ones who spoke, but it was the Holy Spirit who "taught them what to say." Could any language express more emphatically the most entire inspiration? and, if the Holy Spirit so controlled their utterances when in the presence of "magistrates," is it conceivable that He would do less for them when they were

The Divine Inspiration of the Bible

communicating the mind of God to all future generations on things touching our eternal destiny? Assuredly not. "But those things, which God before had showed by the mouth of all His prophets, that Christ should suffer, He hath so fulfilled" (Acts 3:18). Here the Holy Spirit declares through Peter that it was God who had revealed by the mouth of all His prophets that Israel's Messiah must suffer before the glory should appear. "But that I confess unto thee, that after the way which they call heresy, so worship I the God of my fathers, believing all things which are written in the law and in the prophets" (Acts 24:14). These words clearly evidence the fact that the Apostle Paul had the utmost confidence in the authenticity of the entire contents of the Old Testament. "And my speech and my preaching was not with enticing words of man's wisdom, but in demonstration of the Spirit and of power" (1 Cor. 2:4). Could any man have used such language as this unless he had been fully conscious that he was speaking the very words of God? "The prophecy came not at any time by the will of man: but holy men of God spoke as they were moved by the Holy Spirit" (2 Pet. 1:21). Nothing could possibly be more explicit.

Dr. Gray has strikingly and forcefully stated the necessity of a verbally inspired Bible in the following language:—"An illustration the writer has often used will help to make this clear. A stenographer in a mercantile house was asked by his employer to write as follows:

"Gentlemen: we misunderstood your letter and will not fill your order."

Imagine the employer's surprise, however, when a little later this was set before him for his signature:

"Gentlemen: we misunderstood your letter and will not fill your order."

The mistake was only of a single letter, but it was entirely subversive of his meaning. And yet the thought was given clearly to the stenographer, and the words, too, for that matter, Moreover, the latter was capable and faithful, but he was human, and it is human to err. Had not his employer controlled his expression, down to the very letter, the thought intended to be conveyed would have failed of utterance." So, too, the Holy Spirit had to superintend the writing of the very letter of Scripture in order to guarantee its accuracy and inerrancy.

Many proofs might be given to show the Scriptures are verbally inspired. One line of demonstration appears in the literal and verbal fulfillment of many of the Old Testament prophecies. For example, God made known through Zechariah that the price which Judas should receive for his awful crime was "thirty pieces of silver" (Zech. 11:12). Here then is a clear case where God communicated to one of the prophets not merely an abstract concept but a specific communication. And the above case is only one of many.

Another evidence of verbal inspiration is to be seen in the fact that words are used in Scripture with the most exact precision and discrimination. This is particularly noticeable in connection with the Divine titles. The names Elohim and Jehovah are found on the pages of the Old Testament several thousand times, but they are never employed loosely or used alternately. Each of these names has a definite significance and scope, and were we to substitute the one for the other the beauty and perfection of a multitude of passages would be destroyed. To illustrate: the word "God" occurs all through Genesis 1, but "Lord God" in Genesis 2. Were these two Divine titles reversed here, a flaw and blemish would be the consequence. "God" is the creatorial title, whereas "Lord" implies covenant relationship and shows God's dealings with His own people. Hence, in Genesis 1, "God" is used, and in Genesis 2, "Lord God" is employed, and all through the remainder of the Old Testament these two Divine titles are used discriminatively and in harmony with the meaning of their first mention. One or two other examples must suffice. "And they went in unto Noah into the ark, two and two of all flesh, wherein is the breath of life. And they that went in, went in male and female of all flesh, as God had commanded him"—"God" because it was the Creator commanding, with respect to His creatures, as such; but, in the remainder of the same verse, we read, "and the Lord shut him in" (Gen. 7:16), because God's action here toward Noah was based upon covenant relationship. When going forth to meet Goliath David said, "This day will the Lord deliver thee into mine hand (because David was in covenant relationship with Him); and I will smite thee, and take thine head from thee; and I will give the carcasses of the host of the Philistines this day unto the fowls of the air, and to the wild beasts of the earth; that all the earth (which was not in covenant relation with Him) may know that there is a God in Israel. And all this assembly (which were in covenant relationship with Him) shall know that the Lord saveth not with sword and spear" etc.

(1 Sam. 17:46-47). Once more: "And it came to pass, when the captains of the chariots saw Jehoshaphat, that they said, It is the king of Israel. Therefore they compassed about him to fight: but Jehoshaphat cried out, and the Lord helped him; and God moved them (the Syrians) to depart from him" (2 Chron. 18:31). And thus it is all through the Old Testament.

The above line of argument might be extended indefinitely. There are upwards of fifty Divine titles in the Old Testament which are used more than once, each of which has a definite signification, each of which has its meaning hinted at in its first mention, and each of which is used subsequently in harmony with its original purport. They are never used loosely or interchangeably. In every place where they occur there is a reason for each variation. Such titles are the Most High, the Almighty, the God of Israel, the God of Jacob, the Lord our Righteousness, etc., etc., are not used haphazardly, but in every case in harmony with their original meaning and as the best suited to the context. The same is true in connection with the names of our Lord in the New Testament. In some passages He is referred to as Christ, in others as Jesus, Jesus Christ, Christ Jesus, Lord Jesus Christ. In every instance there is a reason for each variation, and in every case the Holy Spirit has seen to it that they are employed with uniform significance. The same is true of the various names given to the great adversary. In some places he is termed Satan, in others the devil etc., etc.; but the different terms are used with unerring precision throughout. A further illustration is furnished by the father of Joseph. In his earlier life he was always termed Jacob, later he received the name of Israel, but after this, sometimes we read of Jacob and sometimes of Israel. Whatever is predicted of Jacob refers to the acts of the "old man;" whatever is postulated of Israel were the fruits of the "new man." When he doubted it was Jacob who doubted, when he believed God it was Israel who exercised faith. Accordingly, we read, "And when Jacob had made an end of commanding his sons, he gathered up his feet into the bed, and yielded up the ghost" (Gen. 49:33). But in the next verse but one we are told, "And Joseph commanded his servants the physicians to embalm his father: and the physicians embalmed Israel (Gen. 50:2)!! Here then we see the marvelous verbal precision and perfection of Holy Scripture.

The most convincing of all the proofs and arguments for the verbal inspiration of the Scriptures is the fact that the Lord Jesus Christ regarded them and treated them as such. He Himself submitted to their authority. When assaulted by Satan, three times He replied, "It is written," and it is particularly to be noted that the point of each of His quotations and the force of each reply lay in a single word—"Man shall not live by bread alone" etc.; "Thou shalt not tempt the Lord thy God;" "Thou shalt worship the Lord thy God, and him only shalt thou serve." When tempted by the Pharisees, who asked Him, "Is it lawful for a man to put away his wife for every cause?" He answered, "Have ye not read?" etc. (Matt. 19:4-5). To the Sadducees He said, "Ye do err, not knowing the Scriptures" (Matt. 22:29). On another occasion He accused the Pharisees of "Making the Word of God of none effect through their tradition" (Mark 7:13). On another occasion, when speaking of the Word of God, He declared "The Scripture cannot be broken" (John 10:35). Sufficient has been adduced to show that the Lord Jesus regarded the Scriptures as the Word of God in the most absolute sense. In view of this fact let Christians beware of detracting in the smallest degree from the perfect and full inspiration of the Holy Scriptures.

CHAPTER FOURTEEN
APPLICATION OF THE ARGUMENT

What is our attitude towards God's Word? The knowledge that the Scriptures are inspired by the Holy Spirit involves definite obligations. Our conception of the authority of the Bible determines our attitude and measures our responsibility. If the Bible is a Divine revelation what follows?

I. We Need to Seek God's Forgiveness.

If it were announced upon reliable authority that on a certain date in the near future an angel from heaven would visit New York and would deliver a sermon upon the invisible world, the future destiny of man, or the secret of deliverance from the power of sin, what an audience he would command! There is no building in that city large enough to accommodate the crowd which would throng to hear him. If upon the next day, the newspapers were to give a verbatim report of his discourse, how eagerly it would be read! And yet, we have between the covers of the Bible not merely an angelic communication but a Divine revelation. How great then is our wickedness if we undervalue and despise it! And yet we do.

We need to confess to God our sin of neglecting His Holy Word. We have time enough—we take time—to read the writings of fellow sinners, yet we have little or no time for the Holy Scriptures. The Bible is a series of Divine love letters, and yet many of God's people have scarcely broken the seals. God complained of old, "I have written to him the great things of My law, but they were counted as a strange thing" (Hos. 8:12). To neglect God's gift is to despise the Giver. To neglect God's Word is virtually to tell Him that He made a mistake in being at so much trouble to communicate it. To prefer the writings of man is to insult the Almighty. To say that human writings are more interesting is to impugn the wisdom of the Most High and is a terrible indictment against our own evil hearts. To neglect God's Word is to sin against its Author, for He has commanded us to read, study, and search it.

If the Bible is the Word of God then—

II. It is the Final Court of Appeal.

It is not a question of what I think, or of what anyone else thinks—it is, What saith the Scriptures? It is not a matter of what any church or creed teaches—it is, What teaches the Bible? God has spoken, and that ends the matter: "Forever, O Lord, Thy Word is settled in heaven." Therefore, it is for me to bow to His authority, to submit to His Word, to cease all quibbling and cry, "Speak, Lord, for Thy servant heareth." Because the Bible is God's Word, it is the final court of appeal in all things pertaining to doctrine, duty, and deportment.

This was the position taken by our Lord Himself. When tempted by Satan, He declined to argue with him, He refused to overwhelm him with the force of His superior wisdom, He scorned to crush him with a putting forth of His almighty power—"It is written" was His defense for each assault. At the beginning of His public ministry, when He went to Nazareth where most of His thirty years had been lived, He performed no wonderful miracle but entered the synagogue, read from the Prophet Isaiah and said, "This day is this Scripture fulfilled in your ears" (Luke 4:21). In His teaching upon the Rich Man and Lazarus, He insisted that "If they hear not Moses and the prophets, neither will they be persuaded, though one rose from the dead" (Luke 16:31)—thus signifying that the authority of the written Word is of greater weight and worth than the testimony and appeal of miracles. When vindicating before the Jews His claim of Deity (John 5) He appealed to the testimony of John the Baptist (vs. 32), to His own works (vs. 36), to the Father's own witness—at His baptism (vs. 37), and then—as tho they were the climax—He said— "Search the Scriptures...they are they which testify of Me" (vs. 39).

This was the position taken by the Apostles. When Peter would justify the speaking with other tongues, he appealed to the Prophet Joel (Acts 2:16). When seeking to prove to the Jews that Jesus of Nazareth was their Messiah, and that He had risen again from the dead, he appealed to the testimony of the Old Testament (Act 2). When Stephen made his defense before the "counsel" he did little more than review the teaching of Moses and the prophets. When Saul and Barnabas set out on their first missionary journey they "preached the Word of God in the synagogues of the Jews" (Acts 13:5). In his Epistles, the Apostle continually pauses to ask— "What saith the Scripture?" (Rom. 4:3, etc.)—if the Scripture gave

The Divine Inspiration of the Bible

a clear utterance upon the subject under discussion that ended the matter: against their testimony there was no appeal.

If the Bible is the Word of God—then

III. It is the Ultimate Standard for Regulating Conduct.

How can man be just with God? or how can he be clean that is born of a woman? What must I do to be saved? Where is true and lasting peace and rest to be found? Such are some of the inquiries made by every honest and anxious soul. The reply is—Search the Scriptures: Look and see. How shall I best employ my time and talents? How shall I discover what is well-pleasing to my Maker? How am I to know what is the path of duty? And again the answer is—What teaches the Word of God?

No one who possesses a copy of the Bible can legitimately plead ignorance of God's will. The Scriptures leave us without excuse. A lamp has been provided for our feet and the pathway of righteousness is clearly marked out. A chart has been given to the sailors on time's sea, and it is their own fault if they fail to arrive at the heavenly port. In the day of judgment the Books will be opened and out of these Books men will be judge, and one of these Books will be the Bible. In His written Word God has revealed His mind, expressed His will, communicated His requirements; and woe to the man or woman who takes not the necessary time to discover what these are.

If the Bible is the Word of God then—

IV. It is a Sure Foundation for Our Faith.

Man craves for certainty. Speculations and hypotheses are insufficient where eternal issues are at stake. When I come to lay my head upon my dying pillow, I want something surer than a "perhaps" to rest it upon. And thank God I have it. Where? In the Holy Scriptures. I know that my Redeemer liveth. I know that I have passed from death unto life. I know that I shall be made like Christ and dwell with Him in glory throughout the endless ages of eternity. How do I know? Because God's Word says so, and I want nothing more.

The Bible gives forth no uncertain sound. It speaks with absolute assurance, dogmatism, and finality. Its promises are certain for they are promises of Him who cannot lie. Its testimony is reliable for it is the inerrant Word of the Living God. Its teachings are trustworthy for they are a communication the Omniscient. The believer then has a sure foundation on which to rest, an impregnable rock on which to build his hopes. For his present peace and for his future prospects he has a, "Thus saith the Lord," and that is sufficient.

If the Bible is the Word of God then—

V. It has Unique Claims Upon Us.

A unique book deserves and demands unique attention. Like Job, we ought to be able to say, "I have esteemed the words of His mouth more than my necessary food." If history teaches us anything at all, it teaches that those nations which have most honored God's Word have been most honored by God. And what is true of the nation is equally true of the family and of the individual. The greatest intellects of the ages have drawn their inspiration from the Scripture of Truth. The most eminent statesmen have testified to the value and importance of Bible study. Benjamin Franklin said: "Young man, my advice to you is that you cultivate an acquaintance with and firm belief in the Holy Scriptures, for this is your certain interest." Thomas Jefferson gave it as his opinion, "I have said and always will say, that the studious perusal of the Sacred Volume will make better citizens, better fathers, and better husbands."

When the late Queen Victoria was asked the secret of England's greatness, she took down a copy of the Scriptures, and pointing to the Bible she said, "That Book explains the power of Great Britain." Daniel Webster once affirmed, "If we abide by the principles taught in the Bible, our country will go on prospering and to prosper; but, if we and our posterity neglect its instructions and authority, no man can tell how sudden a catastrophe may overwhelm us and bury all our glory in profound obscurity. The Bible is the Book of all others for lawyers as well as divines, and I pity the man who cannot find in it a rich supply of thought and rule of conduct."

When Sir Walter Scott lay dying he summoned to his side his man in waiting and said, "Read to me out of the Book." Which book? answered his servant. "There is only one Book," was the dying man's response—"The Bible!" The Bible is the Book to live by and the Book to die by. Therefore read it to be wise, believe it to be safe, practice it to be holy. As another has said: "Know it in the head, store it in the heart, show it in the life, sow it in the world."

"All Scripture is given by inspiration of God, and is profitable for doctrine, for reproof, for correction, for instruction in righteousness: that the man of God may be perfect, thoroughly furnished unto all good works" (2 Tim. 3:16-17).

Profiting From
The Word

Arthur W. Pink

Contents

Chapter 1 The Scriptures and Sin	87
Chapter 2 The Scriptures and God	94
Chapter 3 The Scriptures and Christ	103
Chapter 4 The Scriptures and Prayer	111
Chapter 5 The Scriptures and Good Works	120
Chapter 6 The Scriptures and Obedience	128
Chapter 7 The Scriptures and the World	136
Chapter 8 The Scriptures and the Promises	143
Chapter 9 The Scriptures and Joy	151
Chapter 10 The Scriptures and Love	159

Chapter 1
The Scriptures and Sin

There is grave reason to believe that much Bible reading and Bible study of the last few years has been of no spiritual profit to those who engaged in it. Yea, we go further; we greatly fear that in many instances it has proved a curse rather than a blessing. This is strong language, we are well aware, yet no stronger than the case calls for. Divine gifts may be misused, and Divine mercies abused. That this has been so in the present instance is evident by the fruits produced. Even the natural man may (and often does) take up the study of the Scriptures with the same enthusiasm and pleasure as he might of the sciences. Where this is the case, his store of knowledge is increased, and so also is his pride. Like a chemist engaged in making interesting experiments, the intellectual searcher of the Word is quite elated when he makes some discovery in it; but the joy of the latter is no more spiritual than would be that of the former. Again, just as the successes of the chemist generally increase his sense of self-importance and cause him to look with disdain upon others more ignorant than himself, so alas, is it often the case with those who have investigated Bible numerics, typology, prophecy and other such subjects.

The Word of God may be taken up from various motives. Some read it to satisfy their literary pride. In certain circles it has become both the respectable and popular thing to obtain a general acquaintance with the contents of the Bible simply because it is regarded as an educational defect to be ignorant of them. Some read it to satisfy their sense of curiosity, as they might any other book of note. Others read it to satisfy their sectarian pride. They consider it a duty to be well versed in the particular tenets of their own denomination and so search eagerly for proof-texts in support of "our doctrines." Yet others read it for the purpose of being able to argue successfully with those who differ from them. But in all this there is no thought of God, no yearning for spiritual edification, and therefore no real benefit to the soul.

Of what, then, does a true profiting from the Word consist? Does not 2 Timothy 3:16,17 furnish a clear answer to our question? There we read, "All scripture is given by inspiration of God, and is profitable for doctrine, for reproof, for correction, for instruction in righteousness: that the man of God may be perfect, thoroughly furnished unto all good works." Observe what is here omitted: the Holy Scriptures are given us not for intellectual gratification and carnal speculation, but to furnish unto "all good works," and that by teaching, reproving, correcting us. Let us endeavor to amplify this by the help of other passages.

1. An individual is spiritually profited when the Word convicts him of sin. This is its first office: to reveal our depravity, to expose our vileness, to make known our wickedness. A man's moral life may be irreproachable, his dealings with his fellows faultless; but when the Holy Spirit applies the Word to his heart and conscience, opening his sin-blinded eyes to see his relation and attitude to God, he cries, "Woe is me, for I am undone." It is in this way that each truly saved soul is brought to realize his need of Christ. "They that are whole need not a physician, but they that are sick" (Luke 5:31). Yet it is not until the Spirit applies the Word in Divine power that any individual is made to feel that he is sick, sick unto death.

Such conviction that brings home to the heart the awful ravages which sin has wrought in the human constitution is not to be restricted to the initial experience which immediately precedes conversion. Each time that God blesses His Word to my heart, I am made to feel how far, far short I come of the standard which He has set before me, namely, "Be ye holy in all manner of conversation" (1 Pet. 1:15). Here, then, is the first test to apply: as I read of the sad failures of different ones in Scripture, does it make me realize how sadly like unto them I am? As I read of the blessed and perfect life of Christ, does it make me recognize how terribly unlike Him I am?

2. An individual is spiritually profited when the Word makes him sorrow over sin. Of the stony-ground hearer it is said that he "heareth the word, and anon with joy receiveth it; yet hath he not root in himself" (Matt. 13:20,21); but of those who were convicted under the preaching of Peter it is recorded that they were pricked in their heart (Acts 2:37). The same contrast exists today. Many will listen to a flowery sermon, or an address on "dispensational

truth" that displays oratorical powers or exhibits the intellectual skill of the speaker, but which, usually, contains no searching application to the conscience. It is received with approbation, but no one is humbled before God or brought into a closer walk with Him through it. But let a faithful servant of the Lord (who by grace is not seeking to acquire a reputation for his "brilliance") bring the teaching of Scripture to bear upon character and conduct, exposing the sad failures of even the best of God's people, and, though the crowd will despise the messenger, the truly regenerate will be thankful for the message which causes them to mourn before God and cry, "Oh, wretched man that I am." So it is in the private reading of the Word. It is when the Holy Spirit applies it in such a way that I am made to see and feel my inward corruption's that I am really blessed.

What a word is that in Jeremiah 31:19: "After that I was instructed, I smote upon my thigh: I was ashamed, yea, even confounded." Do you, my reader, know anything of such an experience? Does your study of the Word produce a broken heart and lead to a humbling of yourself before God? Does it convict you of your sins in such a way that you are brought to daily repentance before Him? The paschal lamb had to be eaten with "bitter herbs" (Ex. 12:8); so as we really feed on the Word, the Holy Spirit makes it "bitter" to us before it becomes sweet to our taste. Note the order in Revelation 10:9, "And I went unto the angel, and said unto him, Give me the little book. And he said unto me, Take it, and eat it up; and it shall make thy belly bitter, but it shall be in thy mouth sweet as honey." This is ever the experimental order: there must be mourning before comfort (Matt. 5:4); humbling before exalting (1 Pet. 5:6).

3. An individual is spiritually profited when the Word leads to confession of sin. The Scriptures are profitable for "reproof" (2 Tim. 3:16), and an honest soul will acknowledge its faults. Of the carnal it is said, "For every one that loveth evil hateth the light, neither cometh to the light, lest his deeds should be reproved" (John 3:20). "God be merciful to me a sinner" is the cry of a renewed heart, and every time we are quickened by the Word (Ps. 119) there is a fresh revealing to us and a fresh owning by us of our transgressions before God. "He that covereth his sins shall not prosper: but whoso confesseth and forsaketh them shall have mercy" (Prov. 28:13). There can be no spiritual prosperity or fruit-

fulness (Ps. 1:3) while we conceal within our breasts our guilty secrets; only as they are freely owned before God, and that in detail, shall we enjoy His mercy.

There is no real peace for the conscience and no rest for the heart while we bury the burden of unconfessed sin. Relief comes when it is fully unbosomed to God. Mark well the experience of David, "When I kept silence, my bones waxed old through my roaring all the day long. For day and night thy hand was heavy upon me: my moisture is turned into the drought of summer" (Ps. 33:3,4). Is this figurative but forcible language unintelligible unto you? Or does your own spiritual history explain it? There is many a verse of Scripture which no commentary save that of personal experience can satisfactorily interpret. Blessed indeed is the immediate sequel here: "I acknowledged my sin unto thee, and mine iniquity have I not hid. I said, I will confess my transgressions unto the Lord; and thou forgavest the iniquity of my sin" (Ps. 32:5).

4. An individual is spiritually profited when the Word produces in him a deeper hatred of sin. "Ye that love the Lord, hate evil" (Ps. 97: 10). "We cannot love God without hating that which He hates. We are not only to avoid evil, and refuse to continue in it, but we must be up in arms against it, and bear towards it a hearty indignation" (C. H. Spurgeon). One of the surest tests to apply to the professed conversion is the heart's attitude towards sin. Where the principle of holiness has been planted, there will necessarily be a loathing of all that is unholy. If our hatred of evil be genuine, we are thankful when the Word reproves even the evil which we suspected not.

This was the experience of David: "Through thy precepts I get understanding: therefore I hate every false way" (Ps. 119:128). Observe well, it is not merely "I abstain from," but "I hate"; not only "some" or "many," but "every false way"; and not only "every evil," but "every false way." "Therefore I esteem all thy precepts concerning all things to be right, and I hate every false way" (Ps. 119:128). But it is the very opposite with the wicked: "Seeing thou hatest instruction, and castest my words behind thee" (Ps. 50:17). In Proverbs 8:13, we read, "The fear of the Lord is to hate evil," and this godly fear comes through reading the Word: see Deuteronomy 17:18, 19. Rightly has it been said, "Till sin be hated, it cannot be mortified; you will never cry against it, as the Jews did against Christ, Crucify it, Crucify it, till sin be really abhorred as He was"

(Edward Reyner, 1635).

5. An individual is spiritually profited when the Word causes a forsaking of sin. "Let everyone that nameth the name of Christ depart from iniquity" (2 Tim. 2: 19). The more the Word is read with the definite object of discovering what is pleasing and what is displeasing to the Lord, the more will His will become known; and if our hearts are right with Him the more will our ways be conformed thereto. There will be a "walking in the truth" (3 John 4). At the close of 2 Corinthians 6 some precious promises are given to those who separate themselves from unbelievers. Observe, there, the application which the Holy Spirit makes of them. He does not say, "Having therefore these promises, be comforted and become complacent thereby," but "Having therefore these promises, dearly beloved, let us cleanse ourselves from all filthiness of the flesh and spirit" (2 Cor. 7:1).

"Now ye are clean through the word which I have spoken unto you" (John 15:3). Here is another important rule by which we should frequently test ourselves: Is the reading and studying of God's Word producing a purging of my ways? Of old the question was asked, "Wherewithal shall a young man cleanse his way?" and the Divine answer is "by taking heed thereto according to thy word." Yes, not simply by reading, believing, or memorizing it, but by the personal application of the Word to our "way." It is by taking heed to such exhortations as "Flee fornication" (1 Cor. 6:18), "Flee from idolatry" (1 Cor. 10:14). "Flee these things"—a covetous love for money (1 Tim. 6:11), "Flee also youthful lusts" (2 Tim. 2:22), that the Christian is brought into practical separation from evil; for sin has not only to be confessed but "forsaken" (Prov. 28: 13).

6. An individual is spiritually profited when the Word fortifies against sin. The Holy Scriptures are given to us not only for the purpose of revealing our innate sinfulness, and the many, many ways in which we "come short of the glory of God" (Rom 3:23), but also to teach us how to obtain deliverance from sin, how to be kept from displeasing God. "Thy word have I hid in mine heart, that I might not sin against thee" (Ps. 119:11). This is what each of us is required to do: "Receive, I pray thee, the law from his mouth, and lay up his words in thine heart" (Job 22:22). It is particularly the commandments, the warnings, the exhortations, we need to make our own and to treasure; to memorize them, meditate upon them, pray over them, and put them into practice. The only effective way

of keeping a plot of ground from being overgrown by weeds is to sow good seed therein: "Overcome evil with good" (Rom 12:21). So the more Christ's Word dwells in us "richly" (Col. 3: 16), the less room will there be for the exercise of sin in our hearts and lives.

It is not sufficient merely to assent to the veracity of the Scriptures, they require to be received into the affections. It is unspeakably solemn to note that the Holy Spirit specifies as the ground of apostasy, "because the love of the truth they received not" (2 Thess. 2:10, Greek). "If it lie only in the tongue or in the mind, only to make it a matter of talk and speculation, it will soon be gone. The seed which lies on the surface, the fowls in the air will pick up. Therefore hide it deeply; let it get from the ear into the mind, from the mind into the heart; let it soak in further and further. It is only when it hath a prevailing sovereignty in the heart that we receive it in the love of it—when it is dearer than our dearest lust, then it will stick to us" (Thomas Manton).

Nothing else will preserve from the infections of this world, deliver from the temptations of Satan, and be so effective a preservative against sin, as the Word of God received into the affections, "The law of his God is in his heart; none of his steps shall slide" (Ps. 37:31). As long as the truth is active within us, stirring the conscience, and is really loved by us, we shall be kept from falling. When Joseph was tempted by Potiphar's wife, he said, "How then can I do this great wickedness, and sin against God?" (Gen. 39:9). The Word was in his heart, and therefore had prevailing power over his lusts. The ineffable holiness, the mighty power of God, who is able both to save and to destroy. None of us knows when he may be tempted: therefore it is necessary to be prepared against it. "Who among you will give ear . . . and hear for the time to come?" Isa. 42:23). Yes, we are to anticipate the future and be fortified against it, by storing up the Word in our hearts for coming emergencies.

7. An individual is spiritually profited when the Word causes him to practice the opposite of sin. "Sin is the transgression of the law" (1 John 3:4). God says "Thou shalt," sin says "I will not"; God says "Thou shalt not," sin says "I will." Thus, sin is rebellion against God, the determination to have my own way (Isa. 53:6). Therefore sin is a species of anarchy in the spiritual realm, and may be likened unto the waving of the red flag in the face of God. Now the opposite of sinning against God is submission to Him, as

the opposite of lawlessness is subjection to the law. Thus, to practice the opposition of sin is to walk in the path of obedience. This is another chief reason why the Scriptures were given: to make known the path which is pleasing to God for us. They are profitable not only for reproof and correction, but also for "instruction in righteousness."

Here, then, is another important rule by which we should frequently test ourselves. Are my thoughts being formed, my heart controlled, and my ways and works regulated by God's Word? This is what the Lord requires: "Be ye doers of the word, and not hearers only, deceiving your own selves" (Jas. 1:22). This is how gratitude to and affection for Christ are to be expressed: "If ye love me, keep my commandments" (John 14:15). For this, Divine assistance is needed. David prayed, "Make me to go in the path of thy commandments" (Ps. 119:35). "We need not only light to know our way, but a heart to walk in it. Direction is necessary because of the blindness of our minds; and the effectual impulsions of grace are necessary because of the weakness of our hearts. It will not answer our duty to have a naked notion of truths, unless we embrace and pursue them" (Manton). Note it is "the path of thy commandments": not a self-chosen course, but a definitely marked one; not a public "road," but a private "path."

Let both writer and reader honestly and diligently measure himself, as in the presence of God, by the seven things here enumerated. Has your study of the Bible made you more humble, or more proud—proud of the knowledge you have acquired? Has it raised you in the esteem of your fellow men, or has it led you to take a lower place before God? Has it produced in you a deeper abhorrence and loathing of self, or has it made you more complacent? Has it caused those you mingle with, or perhaps teach, to say, I wish I had your knowledge of the Bible; or does it cause you to pray, Lord give me the faith, the grace, the holiness Thou hast granted my friend, or teacher? 'Meditate upon these things; give thyself wholly to them; that thy profiting may appear unto all' (1 Tim. 6:15).

Arthur W. Pink

Chapter 2
The Scriptures and God

The Holy Scriptures are wholly supernatural. They are a Divine revelation. "All scripture is given by inspiration of God" (2 Tim. 3:16). It is not merely that God elevated men's minds, but that He directed their thoughts. It is not simply that He communicated concepts to them, but that He dictated the very words they used. "The prophecy came not in old time by the will of man: but holy men of God spoke as they were moved by the Holy Spirit" (2 Pet. 1:21). Any human "theory" which denies their verbal inspiration is a device of Satan's, an attack upon God's truth. The Divine image is stamped upon every page. Writings so holy, so heavenly, so awe-producing, could not have been created by man.

The Scriptures make known a supernatural God. That may be a very trite remark, yet today it needs making. The "god" which is believed in by many professing Christians is becoming more and more paganized. The prominent place which "sport" now has in the nation's life, the excessive love of pleasure, the abolition of home-life, the brazen immodesty of women, are so many symptoms of the same disease which brought about the downfall and death of the empires of Babylon, Persia, Greece and Rome. And the twentieth-century idea of God which is entertained by the majority of people in lands nominally "Christian" is rapidly approximating to the character ascribed to the gods of the ancients. In sharp contrast therewith, the God of Holy Writ is clothed with such perfections and vested with such attributes that no mere human intellect could possibly have invented them.

God can only be known by means of a supernatural revelation of Himself. Apart from the Scriptures, even a theoretical acquaintance with Him is impossible. It still holds true that "the world by wisdom knew not God" (1 Cor. 1:21). Where the Scriptures are ignored, God is "the unknown God" (Acts 17:23). But something more than the Scriptures is required before the soul can know

God, know him in a real, personal, vital way. This seems to be recognized by few today. The prevailing practice assumes that a knowledge of God can be obtained through studying the Word, in the same way as a knowledge of chemistry may be secured by mastering its textbooks. An intellectual knowledge of God maybe; not so a spiritual one. A supernatural God can only be known supernaturally (i.e. known in a manner above that which mere nature can acquire), by a supernatural revelation of Himself to the heart. "God, who commanded the light to shine out of darkness, hath shined in our hearts, to give the light of the knowledge of the glory of God in the face of Jesus Christ" (2 Cor. 4:6). The one who has been favored with this supernatural experience has learned that only "in thy light shall we see light" (Ps. 36:9).

God can only be known through a supernatural faculty. Christ made this clear when He said, "Except a man be born again, he cannot see the kingdom of God" (John 3:3). The unregenerate have no spiritual knowledge of God. "The natural man receiveth not the things of the Spirit of God: for they are foolishness unto him: neither can he know them, because they are spiritually discerned" (1 Cor. 2:14). Water, of itself, never rises above its own level. So the natural man is incapable of perceiving that which transcends mere nature. "This is life eternal, that they might know thee the only true God" (John 17:3). Eternal life must be imparted before the "true God" can be known. Plainly is this affirmed in 1 John 5:20, "We know that the Son of God is come, and hath given us an understanding, that we may know Him that is true." Yes, an "understanding," a spiritual understanding, by new creation, must be given before God can be known in a spiritual way.

A supernatural knowledge of God produces a supernatural experience, and this is something to which multitudes of church members are total strangers. Most of the "religion" of the day is but a touching up of "old Adam." it is merely a garnishing of sepulchers full of corruption. It is an outward "form." Even where there is a sound creed, only too often it is a dead orthodoxy. Nor should this be wondered at. It has ever been thus. It was so when Christ was here upon earth. The Jews were very orthodox. At that time they were free from idolatry. The temple stood at Jerusalem, the Law was expounded, Jehovah was worshipped. And yet Christ said to them, "He that sent me is true, whom ye know not." (John 7:28). "Ye neither know me, nor my Father: if ye had known me, ye should have known my Father also" (John 8:19). "It is my Father that honoreth me; of whom ye say, that he is your God. Yet ye have not known him" (John 8:54,55). And mark it well, this is said to a people who had the Scriptures, searched them diligently, and venerated them as God's Word! They were well acquainted with God theoretically, but a spiritual knowledge of Him they had not.

As it was in the Jewish world, so it is in Christendom. Multitudes who "believe" in the Holy Trinity are completely devoid of a supernatural or spiritual knowledge of God. How are we so sure of this? In this way: the character of the fruit reveals the character of the tree that bears it; the nature of the waters makes known the nature of the fountain from which they flow. A supernatural knowledge of God produces a supernatural experience, and a supernatural experience results in supernatural fruit. That is to say, God actually dwelling in the heart revolutionizes, transforms the life. There is that brought forth which mere nature cannot produce, yea, that which is directly contrary thereto. And this is noticeably absent from the lives of perhaps ninety-five out of every hundred now professing to be God's children. There is nothing in the life of the average professing Christian except what can be accounted for on natural grounds. But in the genuine child of God it is far otherwise. He is, in truth, a miracle of grace; he is a "new creature in Christ Jesus" (2 Cor. 5: 17). His experience, his life, is supernatural.

The supernatural experience of the Christian is seen in his attitude toward God. Having within him the life of God, having been made a "partaker of the Divine nature" (2 Pet. 1:4), he necessarily loves God, loves the things of God, loves what God loves; and, contrariwise, he hates what God hates. This supernatural experience is wrought in him by the Spirit of God, and that by means of the Word of God. The Spirit never works apart from the Word. By that Word He quickens. By that Word He produces conviction of sin. By that Word He sanctifies. By that Word He gives assurance. By that Word He makes the saint to grow. Thus each one of us may ascertain the extent to which we are profiting from our reading and studying of the Scriptures by the effects which they are, through the Spirit's application of them, producing in us. Let us enter now into details. He who is truly and spiritually profiting from the Scriptures has:

1. A clearer recognition of God's claims. The great controversy

between the Creator and the creature has been whether He or they should be God, whether His wisdom or theirs should be the guiding principle of their actions, whether His will or theirs should be supreme. That which brought about the fall of Lucifer was his resentment at being in subjection to his Maker:

"Thou hast said in thine heart, I will ascend into heaven, I will exalt my throne above the stars of God . . . I will be like the most High" (Isa. 14:13, 14). The lie of the serpent which lured our first parents to their destruction was, "Ye shall be as gods" (Gen. 3:5). And ever since then the heart-sentiment of the natural man has been, "Depart from us; for we desire not the knowledge of thy ways. What is the Almighty, that we should serve him?" (Job 21:14,15). "Our lips are our own; who is Lord over us?" (Ps. 12:4). "We are lords; we will come no more unto thee" (Jer. 2:31).

Sin has alienated man from God (Eph. 4: 18). His heart is averse to Him, his will is opposed to His, his mind is at enmity against Him. Contrariwise, salvation means being restored to God: "For Christ also hath once suffered for sins, the just for the unjust, that he might bring us to God" (1 Pet. 3:18).

Legally that has already been done; experimentally it is in the process of accomplishment. Salvation means being reconciled to God; and that involves and includes sin's dominion over us being broken, enmity within us being slain, the heart being won to God. This is what true conversion is; it is a tearing down of every idol, a renouncing of the empty vanities of a cheating world, and taking God for our portion, our ruler, our all in all. Of the Corinthians we read that they "first gave their own selves unto the Lord" (2 Cor. 8:5). The desire and determination of those truly converted is that they "should not henceforth live unto themselves, but unto him which died for them, and rose again" (2 Cor. 5:15).

God's claims are now recognized, His rightful dominion over us is acknowledged, He is owned as God. The converted yield themselves "unto God, as those that are alive from the dead," and their members as "instruments of righteousness unto God" (Rom. 6:13). This is the demand which He makes upon us: to be our God, to be served as such by us; for us to be and do, absolutely and without reserve, whatsoever He demands, surrendering ourselves fully to Him (see Luke 14:26,27,33). It belongs to God as God to legislate, prescribe, determine for us; it belongs to us as a bounded duty to be ruled, governed, disposed of by Him at His pleasure.

To own God as our God is to give Him the throne of our hearts. It is to say in the language of Isaiah 26:13, "O Lord our God, other lords beside thee have had dominion over us: but by thee only will we make mention of thy name." It is to declare with the Psalmist, not hypocritically, but sincerely, "O God, thou art my God; early will I seek thee" (Ps. 63:1). Now it is in proportion as this becomes our actual experience that we profit from the Scriptures. It is in them, and in them alone, that the claims of God are revealed and enforced, and just so far as we are obtaining clearer and fuller views of God's rights, and are yielding ourselves thereto, are we really being blessed.

2. A greater fear of God's majesty. "Let all the earth fear the Lord; let all the inhabitants of the world stand in awe of him" (Ps. 33:8). God is so high above us that the thought of His majesty should make us tremble. His power is so great that the realization of it ought to terrify us. He is so ineffably holy, and His abhorrence of sin is so infinite, that the very thought of wrongdoing ought to fill us with horror. "God is greatly to be feared in the assembly of the saints, and to be had in reverence of all them that are about him" (Ps. 89:7).

"The fear of the Lord is the beginning of wisdom" (Prov. 9:10), and "wisdom" is a right use of "knowledge." Just so far as God is truly known will He be duly feared. Of the wicked it is written, "There is no fear of God before their eyes" (Rom. 3:18). They have no realization of His majesty, no concern for His authority, no respect for His commandments, no alarm that He shall judge them. But concerning His covenant people God has promised, "I will put my fear in their hearts, that they shall not depart from me" (Jer. 32:40). Therefore do they tremble at His Word (Isa. 66:5), and walk softly before Him.

"The fear of the Lord is to hate evil" (Prov. 8:13). And again, "By the fear of the Lord men depart from evil" (Prov. 16: 6). The man who lives in the fear of God is conscious that "the eyes of the Lord are in every place, beholding the evil and the good" (Prov. 15:3), therefore is he conscientious about his private conduct as well as his public. The one who is deterred from committing certain sins because the eyes of men are upon him, and who hesitates not to commit them when alone, is destitute of the fear of God. So too the man who moderates his language when Christians are about him, but does not so at other times, is devoid of God's fear. He has no awe-inspiring consciousness that God sees and hears him at all times. The truly regenerate soul is afraid of disobeying and defying God. Nor does he want to. No, his real and deepest desire is to please Him in all things, at all times, and in all places. His earnest prayer is "Unite my heart to fear thy name" (Ps. 86:11).

Now even the saint has to be taught the fear of God (Ps. 34:11). And here, as ever, it is through the Scriptures that this teaching is given us (Prov. 2:5). It is through them we learn that God's eye is ever upon us, marking our actions, weighing our motives. As the Holy Spirit applies the Scriptures to our hearts, we give increasing heed to that command, "Be thou in the fear of the Lord all the day long" (Prov. 23:17). Thus, just so far as we are awed by God's awful majesty, are made conscious that "Thou God seest me" (Gen. 16:13), and work out our salvation with "fear and trembling" (Phil. 2:12), are we truly profited from our reading and study of the Bible.

3. A deeper reverence for God's commandments. Sin entered this world by Adam's breaking of God's law, and all his fallen children are begotten in his depraved likeness (Gen. 5:3). "Sin is the transgression of the law" (1 John 3:4). Sin is a species of high treason, spiritual anarchy. It is the repudiation of God's dominion, the setting aside of His authority, rebellion against His will. Sin is having our own way. Now salvation is deliverance from sin, from its guilt, from its power as well as its penalty. The same Spirit who convicts of the need of God's grace also convicts of the need of God's government to rule us. God's promise to His covenant people is, "I will put my laws into their mind, and write them in their hearts: and I will be to them a God" (Heb. 8:10).

A spirit of obedience is communicated to every regenerated soul. Said Christ, "If a man love me, he will keep my words" (John 14:23). There is the test: "Hereby we do know that we know him, if we keep his commandments" (1 John 2:3). None of us keeps them perfectly, yet every real Christian both desires and strives to do so. He says with Paul, "I delight in the law of God after the inward man" (Rom. 7:22). He says with the Psalmist, "I have chosen the way of truth," "Thy testimonies have I taken as an heritage forever" (Ps. 119:30,111). And teaching which lowers God's authority, which ignores His commands, which affirms that the Christian is, in no sense, under the Law, is of the Devil, no matter how oily-mouthed his human instrument may be. Christ has redeemed His people from the curse of the Law and not from the command of it;

He has saved them from the wrath of God, but not from His government. "Thou shalt love the Lord thy God with all thine heart" never has been and never will be repealed.

1 Corinthians 9:21, expressly affirms that we are "under the law to Christ." "He that saith he abideth in him ought himself so to walk, even as he walked" (1 John 2:6). And how did Christ "walk"? In perfect obedience to God; in complete subjection to His law, honoring and obeying it in thought and word and deed. He came not to destroy the Law, but to fulfill it (Matt. 5:17). And our love for Him is expressed, not in pleasing emotions or beautiful words, but in keeping His commandments (John 14:15), and the commandments of Christ are the commandments of God (cf. Ex. 20:6). The earnest prayer of the real Christian is, "Make me to go in the path of thy commandments; for therein do I delight" (Ps. 119:35). Just so far as our reading and study of Scripture is, by the Spirit's application, begetting within us a greater love and a deeper respect for and a more punctual keeping of God's commandments, are we really profiting thereby.

4. A firmer trust in God's sufficiency. Whatsoever or whomsoever a man most trusts in is his "god." Some trust in health, others in wealth; some in self, others in their friends. That which characterizes all the unregenerate is that they lean upon an arm of flesh. But the election of grace have their hearts drawn from all creature supports, to rest upon the living God. God's people are the children of faith. The language of their hearts is, "O my God, I trust in thee: let me not be ashamed" (Ps. 25:2). and again, "Though he slay me, yet will I trust in him" (Job 13: 15). They rely upon God to provide, protect and bless them. They look to an unseen resource, count upon an invisible God, lean upon a hidden Arm.

True, there are time when their faith wavers, but though they fall they are not utterly cast down. Though it be not their uniform experience, yet Psalm 56:11 expresses the general state of their souls: "In God have I put my trust: I will not be afraid what man can do unto me." Their earnest prayer is, "Lord, increase our faith." "Faith cometh by hearing, and hearing by the word of God" (Rom. 10:17). Thus, as the Scriptures are pondered, their promises received in the mind, faith is strengthened, confidence in God increased, assurance deepened. By this we may discover whether or not we are profiting from our study of the Bible.

5. A fuller delight in God's perfections. That in which a man most

delights is his "god." The poor worldling seeks satisfaction in his pursuits, pleasures and possessions. Ignoring the Substance, he vainly pursues the shadows. But the Christian delights in the wondrous perfections of God. Really to own God as our God is not only to submit to His scepter, but is to love Him more than the world, to value Him above everything and everyone else. It is to have with the Psalmist an experiential realization that "all my springs are in thee" (Ps. 87:7). The redeemed have not only received a joy from God such as this poor world cannot impart, but they "rejoice in God" (Rom. 5:11); and of this the poor worldling knows nothing. The language of such is "the Lord is my portion" (Lam. 3:24).

Spiritual exercises are irksome to the flesh. But the real Christian says, "It is good for me to draw near to God" (Ps. 73:28). The carnal man has many cravings and ambitions; the regenerate soul declares, "One thing have I desired of the Lord, that will I seek after; that I may dwell in the house of the Lord all the days of my life, to behold the beauty of the Lord" (Ps. 27:4). And why? Because the true sentiment of his heart is, "Whom have I in heaven but thee? and there is none upon earth that I desire beside thee" (Ps. 73:25). Ah, my reader, if your heart has not been drawn out to love and delight in God, then it is still dead toward Him.

The language of the saints is, "Although the fig tree shall not blossom, neither shall fruit be in the vines; the labor of the olive shall fail, and the fields shall yield no meat; the flock shall be cut off from the fold, and there shall be no herd in the stalls: yet I will rejoice in the Lord, I will joy in the God of my salvation" (Hab. 3:17,18). Ah, that is a supernatural experience indeed! Yes, the Christian can rejoice when all his worldly possessions are taken from him (see Heb. 10:34). When he lies in a dungeon with back bleeding, he can still sing praises to God (see Acts 16:25). Thus, to the extent that you are being weaned from the empty pleasures of this world, are learning that there is no blessing outside of God, are discovering that He is the source and sum of all excellency, and your heart is being drawn out to Him, your mind stayed on Him, your soul finding its joy and satisfaction in Him, are you really profiting from the Scriptures.

6. A larger submission to God's providences. It is natural to murmur when things go wrong, it is supernatural to hold our peace (Lev. 10:3). It is natural to be disappointed when our plans miscarry, it is supernatural to bow to His appointments. It is natural

to want our own way, it is supernatural to say, "Not my will, but thine be done." It is natural to rebel when a loved one is taken from us by death, it is supernatural to say from the heart, "The Lord gave, and the Lord hath taken away; blessed be the name of the Lord" (Job 1:21). As God is truly made our portion, we learn to admire His wisdom, and to know that He does all things well. Thus the heart is kept in "perfect peace" as the mind is stayed on Him (Isaiah 26:3). Here, then, is another sure test: if your Bible study is teaching you that God's way is best, if it is causing you to submit unrepiningly to all His dispensations, if you are enabled to give thanks for all things (Eph. 5:20), then are you profiting indeed.

7. A more fervent praise for God's goodness. Praise is the outflow of a heart which finds its satisfaction in God. The language of such a one is, "I will bless the Lord at all times: his praise shall continually be in my mouth" (Ps. 34:1). What abundant cause have God's people for praising Him! Loved with an everlasting love, made sons and heirs, all things working together for their good, their every need supplied, an eternity of bliss assured them, their harps of gladness ought never to be silent. Nor will they be while they enjoy fellowship with Him who is "altogether lovely." The more we are increasing in the knowledge of God (Col. 1:10), the more shall we adore Him. But it is only as the Word dwells in us richly that we are filled with spiritual songs (Col. 3:16) and make melody in our hearts to the Lord. The more our souls are drawn out in true worship, the more we are found thanking and praising our great God, the clearer evidence we give that our study of His word is profiting us.

Chapter 3
The Scriptures and Christ

The order we follow in this series is that of experience. It is not until man is made thoroughly displeased with himself that he begins to aspire after God. The fallen creature deluded by Satan, is self-satisfied till his sin-blinded eyes are opened to get a sight of himself. The Holy Spirit first works in us a sense of our ignorance, vanity, poverty and depravity, before He brings us to perceive and acknowledge that in God alone are to be found true wisdom, real blessedness, perfect goodness and unspotted righteousness. We must be made conscious of our imperfections ere we can really appreciate the Divine perfections. As the perfections of God are contemplated, man becomes still more aware of the infinite distance that separates him from the most High. As he learns something of God's pressing claims upon him, and his own utter inability to meet them, he is prepared to hear and welcome the good news that Another has fully met those claims for all who are led to believe in Him.

"Search the Scriptures," said the Lord Jesus, and then He added, "for. . .they are they which testify of me" (John 5:39). They testify of Him as the only Savior for perishing sinners, as the only Mediator between God and men, as the only one through whom the Father can be approached. They testify to the wondrous perfections of His person, the varied glories of His offices, the sufficiency of His finished work. Apart from the Scriptures, He cannot be known. In them alone He is revealed. When the Holy Spirit takes of the things of Christ and shows them unto His people, in thus making them known to the soul He uses naught but what is written. While it is true that Christ is the key to the Scriptures, it is equally true that only in the Scriptures do we have an opening-up of the "mystery of Christ" (Eph. 3:4).

Now the measure in which we profit from our reading and study of the Scriptures may be ascertained by the extent to which Christ is becoming more real and more precious unto our hearts. To "grow in grace" is defined as and in the knowledge of our Lord and Savior Jesus Christ" (2 Pet. 3:18): the second clause there is not something in addition to the first, but is an explanation of it. To "know" Christ (Phil. 3:10) was the supreme longing and aim of the apostle Paul, a longing and an aim to which he subordinated all other interests. But mark it well, the "knowledge" which is spoken of in these verses is not intellectual but spiritual, not theoretical but experimental, not general but personal. It is a supernatural knowledge, which is imparted to the regenerate heart by the operations of the Holy Spirit, as He interprets and applies to us the Scriptures concerning Him.

Now the knowledge of Christ which the blessed Spirit imparts to the believer through the Scriptures profits him in different ways, according to his varying frames, circumstances and needs. Concerning the bread which God gave to the children of Israel during their wilderness wanderings, it is recorded that "some gathered more, some less" (Ex. 16:17). The same is true in our apprehension of Him of whom the manna was a type. There is that in the wondrous person of Christ which is exactly suited to our every condition, every circumstance, every need, both for time and eternity; but we are slow to realize it, and slower still to act upon it. There is an inexhaustible fullness in Christ (John 1:16) which is available for us to draw from, and the principle regulating the extent to which we become "strong in the grace that is in Christ Jesus" (2 Tim. 2:1) is "According to your faith be it to you" (Matt. 9:29).

1. An individual is profited from the Scriptures when they reveal to him his need of Christ. Man in his natural estate deems himself self-sufficient. True, he has a dim perception that all is not quite right between himself and God, yet has he no difficulty in persuading himself that he is able to do that which will propitiate Him. That lies at the foundation of all man's religion, begun by Cain, in whose "way" (Jude 11) the multitudes still walk. Tell the devout religionist that "they that are in the flesh cannot please God" (Rom. 8:8), and he is at once offended. Press upon him the fact that "all our righteousness's are as filthy rags" (Isa. 64:4), and his hypocritical urbanity at once gives place to anger. So it was when Christ was on earth. The most religious people of all, the Jews, had not sense they were "lost" and in dire need of an almighty Savior.

"They that are whole need not a physician, but they that are sick" (Matt. 9:12). It is the peculiar office of the Holy Spirit, by His application of the Scriptures, to convict sinners of their desperate condition, to bring them to see that their state is such that "from the sole of the foot even unto the head there is no soundness" in them, but "wounds, and bruises, and putrefying sores" (Isa. 1:6). As the Spirit convicts us of our sins—our ingratitude to God, our murmuring against Him, our wanderings from Him—as He presses upon us the claims of God—His right to our love, obedience and adoration—and all our sad failures to render Him His due, then we are made to recognize that Christ is our only hope, and that, except we flee to Him for refuge, the righteous wrath of God will most certainly fall upon us.

Nor is this to be limited to the initial experience of conversion. The more the Spirit deepens His work of grace in the regenerated soul, the more that individual is made conscious of his pollution, his sinfulness and his vileness; and the more does he discover his need of and learn to value that precious, precious blood which cleanses from all sin. The Spirit is here to glorify Christ, and one chief way in which He does so is by opening wider and wider the eyes of those for whom He died, to see how suited Christ is for such wretched, foul, hell-deserving creatures. Yes, the more we are truly profiting from our reading of the Scriptures, the more do we feel our need of Him.

2. An individual is profited from the Scriptures when they make Christ more real to him. The great mass of the Israelitish nation saw nothing more than the outward shell in the rites and ceremonies which God gave them, but a regenerated remnant were privileged to behold Christ Himself. "Abraham rejoiced to see my day" said Christ (John 8:56). Moses esteemed "the reproach of Christ" greater riches than the treasures of Egypt (Heb. 11:16). So it is in Christendom. To the multitudes Christ is but a name, or at most a historical character. They have no personal dealings with Him, enjoy no spiritual communion with Him. Should they hear one speak in rapture of His excellency they regard him as an enthusiast or a fanatic. To them Christ is unreal, vague, intangible. But with the real Christian it is far otherwise. The language of his heart is,

> I have heard the voice of Jesus,
> Tell me not of aught beside;

Arthur W. Pink

> I have seen the face of Jesus,
> And my soul is satisfied.

Yet such a blissful sight is not the consistent and unvarying experience of the saints. Just as clouds come in between the sun and the earth, so failures in our walk interrupt our communion with Christ and serve to hide from us the light of His countenance. "He that hath my commandments, and keepeth them, he it is that loveth me: and he that loveth me shall be loved of my Father, and I will love him, and will manifest myself to him" (John 14:21). Yes, it is the one who by grace is treading the path of obedience to whom the Lord Jesus grants manifestations of Himself. And the more frequent and prolonged these manifestations are, the more real He becomes to the soul, until we are able to say with Job, "I have heard of thee by the hearing of the ear; but now mine eye seeth thee" (42:5). Thus the more Christ is becoming a living reality to me, the more I am profiting from the Word.

3. An individual is profited from the Scriptures when he becomes more engrossed with Christ's perfections. It is a sense of need which first drives the soul to Christ, but it is the realization of His excellency which draws us to run after Him. The more real Christ becomes to us, the more are we attracted by His perfections. At the beginning He is viewed only as a Savior, but as the Spirit continues to take of the things of Christ and show them unto us we discover that upon His head are "many crowns" (Rev. 19:12). Of old it was said, "His name shall be called Wonderful" (Isa. 9:6). His name signifies all that He is as made known in Scripture. "Wonderful" are His offices, in their number, variety, sufficiency. He is the Friend that sticks closer than a brother, to help in every time of need. He is the great High Priest, who is touched with the feeling of our infirmities. He is the Advocate with the Father, who pleads our cause when Satan accuses us.

Our great need is to be occupied with Christ, to sit at His feet as Mary did, and receive out of His fullness. Our chief delight should be to "consider the Apostle and High Priest of our profession" (Heb. 3:1): to contemplate the various relations which He sustains to us, to meditate upon the many promises He has given, to dwell upon His wondrous and changeless love for us. As we do this, we shall so delight ourselves in the Lord that the siren voices of this world will lose all their charm for us. Ah, my reader, do you know anything about this in your own actual experience? Is Christ the chief among ten thousand to your soul? Has He won your heart? Is it your chief joy to get alone and be occupied with Him? If not, your Bible reading and study has profited you little indeed.

4. An individual is profited from the Scriptures as Christ becomes more precious to him. Christ is precious in the esteem of all true believers (1 Pet. 2:7). They count all things but loss for the excellency of the knowledge of Christ Jesus their Lord (Phil. 3:8). His name to them is as ointment poured forth (Song of Sol. 1:3). As the glory of God that appeared in the wondrous beauty of the temple, and in the wisdom and splendor of Solomon, drew worshippers to him from the uttermost parts of the earth, so the unparalleled excellence of Christ which was prefigured thereby does more powerfully attract the hearts of His people. The Devil knows this full well, therefore is he ceaselessly engaged in blinding the minds of them that believe not, by placing between them and Christ the allures of this world. God permits him to assail the believer also, but it is written, "Resist the devil, and he will flee from you" (James 4:7). Resist him by definite and earnest prayer, entreating the Spirit to draw out your affections to Christ.

The more we are engaged with Christ's perfections, the more we love and adore Him. It is lack of experimental acquaintance with Him that makes our hearts so cold towards Him. But where real and daily fellowship is cultivated the Christian will be able to say with the Psalmist, "Whom have I in heaven but thee? and there is none upon earth that I desire beside thee" (Ps. 73:25). This it is which is the very essence and distinguishing nature of true Christianity. Legalistic zealots may be busily engaged in tithing mint and anise and cummin, they may encompass sea and land to make one proselyte, and yet have no love for God in Christ. It is the heart that God looks at: "My son, give me thine heart" (Prov. 23:26) is His demand. The more precious Christ is to us, the more delight does He have in us.

5. An individual who is profited from the Scriptures has an increasing confidence in Christ. There is "little faith" (Matt. 14:3) and "great faith" (Matt. 8:10). There is the "full assurance of faith" (Heb. 10:22), and trusting in the Lord "with all the heart" (Prov. 3:5). Just as there is growing "from strength to strength" (Ps. 84:7), so we read of "from faith to faith" (Rom. 1:17). The stronger and steadier our faith, the more the Lord Jesus is honored. Even

a cursory reading of the four Gospels reveals the fact that nothing pleased the Savior more than the firm reliance which was placed in Him by the few who really counted upon Him. He Himself lived and walked by faith, and the more we do so the more are the members being conformed to their Head. Above everything else there is one thing to be aimed at and diligently sought by earnest prayer: that our faith may be increased. Of the Thessalonian saints Paul was able to say, "Your faith groweth exceedingly" (2 Thess. 1:3).

Now Christ cannot be trusted at all unless He be known, and the better he is known the more will He be trusted: "And they that know thy name will put their trust in thee" (Ps. 9:10). As Christ becomes more real to the heart, as we are increasingly occupied with His manifold perfections and He becomes more precious to us, confidence in Him is deepened until it becomes as natural to trust Him as it is to breathe. The Christian life is a walk of faith (2 Cor. 5:7), and that very expression denotes a continual progress, an increasing deliverance from doubts and fears, a fuller assurance that all He has promised He will perform. Abraham is the father of all them that believe, and thus the record of his life furnishes an illustration of what a deepening confidence in the Lord signifies. First, at His bare word he turned his back upon all that was dear to the flesh. Second, he went forth in simple dependence on Him and dwelt as a stranger and sojourner in the land of promise, though he never owned a single acre of it. Third, when the promise was made of a seed in his old age, he considered not the obstacles in the way of its fulfillment, but was strong in faith, giving glory to God. Finally, when called on to offer up Isaac, through whom the promises were to be realized, he accounted that God was able to "raise him up, even from the dead" (Heb. 11:19).

In the history of Abraham we are shown how grace is able to subdue an evil heart of unbelief, how the spirit may be victorious over the flesh, how the supernatural fruits of a God-given and God-sustained faith may be brought forth by a man of like passions with us. This is recorded for our encouragement, for us to pray that it may please the Lord to work in us what He wrought in and through the father of the faithful. Nothing more pleases, honors and glorifies Christ than the confiding trust, the expectant confidence and the childlike faith of those to whom He has given every cause to trust Him with all their hearts. And nothing more evidences that we are being profited from the Scriptures than an increasing faith in Christ.

6. An individual is profited from the Scriptures when they beget in him a deepening desire to please Christ. "Ye are not your own, for ye are bought with a price" (1 Cor. 6:19,20) is the first great fact that Christians need to apprehend. Henceforth they are not to "live unto themselves, but unto him which died for them, and rose again" (2 Cor. 5:15). Love delights to please its object, and the more our affections are drawn out to Christ the more shall we desire to honor Him by a life of obedience to His known will. "If a man love me, he will keep my words" (John 14:23). It is not in happy emotions or in verbal professions of devotion, but in the actual assumption of His yoke and the practical submitting to His precepts, that Christ is most honored.

It is at this point particularly that the genuineness of our profession may be tested and proved. Have they a faith in Christ who make no effort to learn His will? What a contempt of the king if his subjects refuse to read his proclamations! Where there is faith in Christ there will be delight in His commandments, and a sorrowing when they are broken by us. When we displease Christ we should mourn over our failure. It is impossible seriously to believe that it was my sins which caused the Son of God to shed His precious blood without my hating them. If Christ groaned under sin, we shall groan too. And the more sincere those groanings be, the more earnestly shall we seek grace for deliverance from all that displeases, and strength to do all that which pleases our blessed Redeemer.

7. An individual is profited from the Scriptures when they cause him to long for the return of Christ. Love can be satisfied with nothing short of a sight of its object. True, even now we behold Christ by faith, yet it is "through a glass, darkly." But at His coming we shall behold Him "face to face" (1 Cor. 13:12). Then will be fulfilled His own words, "Father, I will that they also, whom thou hast given me, be with me where I am: that they may behold my glory, which thou hast given me: for thou lovedst me before the foundation of the world" (John 17:24). Only this will fully meet the longings of His heart, and only this will meet the longings of those redeemed by Him. Only then will He "see of the travail of His soul, and be satisfied" (Isa. 53:11); and "As for me, I will behold thy face in righteousness: I shall be satisfied, when I awake, with Thy likeness" (Ps. 17:15).

Arthur W. Pink

At the return of Christ we shall be done with sin forever. The elect are predestined to be conformed to the image of God's Son, and that Divine purpose will be realized only when Christ receives His people unto Himself. "We shall be like him, for we shall see him as he is" (1 John 3: 2). Never again will our communion with Him be broken, never again shall we groan and moan over our inward corruptions; never again shall we be harassed with unbelief. He will present His Church to Himself a glorious church, not having spot, or wrinkle, or any such thing" (Eph. 5:27). For that hour we eagerly wait. For our Redeemer we lovingly look. The more we yearn for the coming One, the more we are trimming our lamps in earnest expectation of His coming, the more do we give evidence that we are profiting from our knowledge of the Word.

Let the reader and writer honestly search themselves as in the presence of God. Let us seek truthful answers to these questions. Have we a deeper sense of our need of Christ? Is He Himself becoming to us a brighter and living reality? Are we finding increasing delight in being occupied with His perfections? Is Christ Himself becoming daily more precious to us? Is our faith in Him growing so that we confidently trust Him for everything? Are we really seeking to please Him in all the details of our lives? Are we so yearning for Him that we would be filled with joy did we know for certain that He would come during the next twenty-four hours? May the Holy Spirit search our hearts with these pointed questions!

Chapter 4
The Scriptures and Prayer

A prayerless Christian is a contradiction in terms. Just as a stillborn child is a dead one, so a professing believer who does not pray is devoid of spiritual life. Prayer is the breath of the new nature in the saint, as the Word of God is its food. When the Lord would assure the Damascus disciple that Saul of Tarsus had been truly converted, He told him, "Behold, he prayeth" (Acts 9:11). On many occasions had that self-righteous Pharisee bowed his knees before God and gone through his "devotions," but this was the first time he had ever really prayed. This important distinction needs emphasizing in this day of powerless forms (2 Tim. 3:5). They who content themselves with formal addresses to God know Him not; for "the spirit of grace and supplications" (Zech. 12:10) are never separated. God has no dumb children in His regenerated family: "Shall not God avenge his own elect, which cry day and night unto Him?" (Luke 18:7). Yes, "cry" unto Him, not merely "say" their prayers.

But will the reader be surprised when the writer declares it is his deepening conviction that, probably, the Lord's own people sin more in their efforts to pray than in connection with any other thing they engage in? What hypocrisy there is, where there should be reality! What presumptuous demandings, where there should be submissiveness! What formality, where there should be brokenness of heart! How little we really feel the sins we confess, and what little sense of deep need for the mercies we seek! And even where God grants a measure of deliverance from these awful sins, how much coldness of heart, how much unbelief, how much self-will and self-pleasing have we to bewail! Those who have no conscience upon these things are strangers to the spirit of holiness.

Now the Word of God should be our directory in prayer. Alas, how often we have made our own fleshly inclinations the rule of our asking. The Holy Scriptures have been given to us "that the man of God may be perfect, thoroughly furnished unto all good works" (2 Tim. 3:17). Since we are required to "pray in the Spirit" (Jude 20), it follows that our prayers ought to be according to the Scriptures, seeing that He is their Author throughout. It equally follows that according to the measure in which the Word of Christ dwells in us "richly" (Col. 3:16) or sparsely, the more or the less will our petitions be in harmony with the mind of the Spirit, for "out of the abundance of the heart the mouth speaketh" (Matt. 12:34). In proportion as we hide the Word in our hearts, and it cleanses, moulds and regulates our inner man, will our prayers be acceptable in God's sight. Then shall we be able to say, as David did in another connection, "Of thine own have we given thee" (1 Chron. 29:14).

Thus the purity and power of our prayer-life are another index by which we may determine the extent to which we are profiting from our reading and searching of the Scriptures. If our Bible study is not, under the blessing of the Spirit, convicting us of the sin of prayerlessness, revealing to us the place which prayer ought to have in our daily lives, and is actually bringing us to spend more time in the secret place of the Most High; unless it is teaching us how to pray more acceptably to God, how to appropriate His promises and plead them before Him, how to appropriate His precepts and turn them into petitions, then not only has the time we spend over the Word been too little or no soul enrichment, but the very knowledge that we have acquired of its letter will only add to our condemnation in the day to come. "Be ye doers of the word, and not hearers only, deceiving your own selves" (James 1:22) applies to its prayer-admonitions as to everything else in it. Let us now point out seven criteria.

1. We are profited from the Scriptures when we are brought to realize the deep importance of prayer. It is really to be feared that many present-day readers (and even students) of the Bible have no deep convictions that a definite prayer-life is absolutely essential to a daily walking and communing with God, as it is for deliverance from the power of indwelling sin, the seductions of the world, and the assaults of Satan. If such a conviction really gripped their hearts, would they not spend far more time on their faces before God? It is worse than idle to reply, "A multitude of duties which have to be performed crowd out prayer, though much against my wishes." But the fact remains that each of us takes time for any-

thing we deem to be imperative. Who ever lived a busier life than our Savior? Yet who found more time for prayer? If we truly yearn to be suppliants and intercessors before God and use all the available time we now have, He will so order things for us that we shall have more time.

The lack of positive conviction of the deep importance of prayer is plainly evidenced in the corporate life of professing Christians. God has plainly said, "My house shall be called the house of prayer" (Matt. 21:13). Note, not "the house of preaching and singing," but of prayer. Yet, in the great majority of even so-called orthodox churches, the ministry of prayer has become a negligible quantity. There are still evangelistic campaigns, and Bible-teaching conferences, but how rarely one hears of two weeks set apart for special prayer! And how much good do these "Bible conferences" accomplish if the prayer-life of the churches is not strengthened? But when the Spirit of God applies in power to our hearts such words as, "Watch ye and pray, lest ye enter into temptation" (Mark 14:38), "In everything by prayer and supplication with thanksgiving let your requests be made known to God" (Phil. 4:6), "Continue in prayer, and watch in the same with thanksgiving" (Col. 4:2), then are we being profited from the Scriptures.

2. We are profited from the Scriptures when we are made to feel that we know not how to pray. "We know not what we should pray for as we ought" (Rom. 8:26). How very few professing Christians really believe this! The idea most generally entertained is that people know well enough what they should pray for, only they are careless and wicked, and so fail to pray for what they are fully assured is their duty. But such a conception is at direct variance with this inspired declaration in Romans 8:26. It is to be observed that that flesh-humbling affirmation is made not simply of men in general, but of the saints of God in particular, among which the apostle did not hesitate to include himself: "We know not what we should pray for as we ought." If this be the condition of the regenerate, how much more so of the unregenerate! Yet it is one thing to read and mentally assent to what this verse says, but it is quite another to have an experimental realization of it, for the heart to be made to feel that what God requires from us He must Himself work in and through us.

"I often say my prayers,

> But do I ever pray?
> And do the wishes of my heart
> Go with the words I say?
>
> I may as well kneel down
> And worship gods of stone,
> As offer to the living God
> A prayer of words alone"

It is many years since the writer was taught these lines by his mother—now "present with the Lord"—but their searching message still comes home with force to him. The Christian can no more pray without the direct enabling of the Holy Spirit than he can create a world. This must be so, for real prayer is a felt need awakened within us by the Spirit, so that we ask God, in the name of Christ, for that which is in accord with His holy will. "If we ask any thing according to his will, he heareth us" (1 John 5:14). But to ask something which is not according to God's will is not praying, but presuming. True, God's revealed will is made known in His Word, yet not in such a way as a cookery book contains recipes and directions for preparing various dishes. The Scriptures frequently enumerate principles which call for continuous exercise of heart and Divine help to show us their application to different cases and circumstances. Thus we are being profited from the Scriptures when we are taught our deep need of crying "Lord, teach us to pray" (Luke 11:1), and are actually constrained to beg Him for the spirit of prayer.

3. We are profited from the Scriptures when we are made conscious of our need of the Spirit's help. First, that He may make known to us our real wants. Take, for example, our temporal needs. How often we are in some external strait; things from without press hard upon us, and we long to be delivered from these trials and difficulties. Surely here we "know" of ourselves what to pray for. No, indeed; far from it! The truth is that, despite our natural desire for relief, so ignorant are we, so dull is our discernment, that (even where there is an exercised conscience) we know not what submission unto His pleasure God may require, or how He may sanctify these afflictions to our inward good. Therefore, God calls the petitions of most who seek for relief from external trials "howlings," and not a crying unto Him with the heart (see Hos. 7:14). "For who knoweth what is good for man in this life?"

(Eccles. 6:12). Ah, heavenly wisdom is needed to teach us our temporal "needs" so as to make them a matter of prayer according to the mind of God.

Perhaps a few words need to be added to what has just been said. Temporal things may be scripturally prayed for (Matt. 6:11, etc.), but with this threefold limitation. First, incidentally and not primarily, for they are not the things which Christians are principally concerned in (Matt. 6:33). It is heavenly and eternal things (Col. 3:1) which are to be sought first and foremost, as being of far greater importance and value than temporal things. Second, subordinately, as a means to an end. In seeking material things from God it should not be in order that we may be gratified, but as an aid to our pleasing Him better. Third, submissively, not dictatorially, for that would be the sin of presumption. Moreover, we know not whether any temporal mercy would really contribute to our highest good (Ps. 106:18), and therefore we must leave it with God to decide.

We have inward wants as well as outward. Some of these may be discerned in the light of conscience, such as the guilt and defilement of sin, of sins against light and nature and the plain letter of the law. Nevertheless, the knowledge which we have of ourselves by means of the conscience is so dark and confused that, apart from the Spirit, we are in no way able to discover the true fountain of cleansing. The things about which believers do and ought to treat primarily with God in their supplications are the inward frames and spiritual dispositions of their souls. Thus, David was not satisfied with confessing all known transgressions and his original sin (Ps. 51:1-5), nor yet with an acknowledgment that none could understand his errors, whence he desired to be cleansed from "secret faults" (Ps. 19:12); but he also begged God to undertake the inward searching of his heart to find out what was amiss in him (Ps. 139:23, 24), knowing that God principally requires "truth in the inward parts" (Ps. 51:6). Thus, in view of I Corinthians 2: 10-12, we should definitely seek the Spirit's aid that we may pray acceptably to God.

4. We are profited from the Scriptures when the Spirit teaches us the right end in praying. God has appointed the ordinance of prayer with at least a threefold design. First, that the great triune God might be honored, for prayer is an act of worship, a paying homage; to the Father as the Giver, in the Son's name, by whom

alone we may approach Him, by the moving and directing power of the Holy Spirit. Second, to humble our hearts, for prayer is ordained to bring us into the place of dependence, to develop within us a sense of our helplessness, by owning that without the Lord we can do nothing, and that we are beggars upon His charity for everything we are and have. But how feebly is this realized (if at all) by any of us until the Spirit takes us in hand, removes pride from us, and gives God His true place in our hearts and thoughts. Third, as a means or way of obtaining for ourselves the good things for which we ask.

It is greatly to be feared that one of the principal reasons why so many of our prayers remain unanswered is because we have a wrong, an unworthy end in view. Our Savior said, "Ask, and it shall be given you" (Matt. 7:7): but James affirms of some, "Ye ask, and receive not, because ye ask amiss, that ye may consume it upon your lusts" (James 4:3). To pray for anything, and not expressly unto the end which God has designed, is to "ask amiss," and therefore to no purpose. Whatever confidence we may have in our own wisdom and integrity, if we are left to ourselves our aims will never be suited to the will of God. Unless the Spirit restrains the flesh within us, our own natural and distempered affections intermix themselves in our supplications, and thus are rendered vain. "Whatsoever ye do, do all to the glory of God" (1 Cor. 10:31), (yet none but the Spirit can enable us to subordinate all our desires unto God's glory.

5. We are profited from the Scriptures when we are taught how to plead God's promises. Prayer must be in faith (Rom. 10:14), or God will not hear it. Now faith has respect to God's promises (Heb. 4:1; Rom. 4:21); if, therefore, we do not understand what God stands pledged to give, we cannot pray at all. The promises of God contain the matter of prayer and define the measure of it. What God has promised, all that He has promised, and nothing else, we are to pray for. "Secret things belong unto the Lord our God" (Deut. 29:29), but the declaration of His will and the revelation of His grace belong unto us, and are our rule. There is nothing that we really stand in need of but God has promised to supply it, yet in such a way and under such limitations as will make it good and useful to us. So too there is nothing God has promised but we stand in need of it, or are some way or other concerned in it as members of the mystical body of Christ. Hence, the better we are

acquainted with the Divine promises, and the more we are enabled to understand the goodness, grace and mercy prepared and proposed in them, the better equipped are we for acceptable prayer.

Some of God's promises are general rather than specific; some are conditional, others unconditional; some are fulfilled in this life, others in the world to come. Nor are we able of ourselves to discern which promise is most suited to our particular case and present emergency and need, or to appropriate by faith and rightly plead it before God. Wherefore we are expressly told, "For what man knoweth the things of a man save the spirit of man which is in him? Even so the things of God knoweth no man, but the Spirit of God. Now we have received, not the spirit of the world but the Spirit which is of God; that we might know the things that are freely given to us of God" (1 Cor. 2: 11, 12). Should someone reply, If so much be required unto acceptable praying, if we cannot supplicate God aright without much less trouble than you indicate, few will continue long in this duty, then we answer that such an objector knows not what it is to pray, nor does he seem willing to learn.

6. We are profited from the Scriptures when we are brought to complete submission unto God. As stated above, one of the Divine designs in appointing prayer as an ordinance is that we might be humbled. This is outwardly denoted when we bow the knee before the Lord. Prayer is an acknowledgment of our helplessness, and a looking to Him from whom all our help comes. It is an owning of His sufficiency to supply our every need. It is a making known our requests" (Phil. 4:6) unto God; but requests are very different from demands. "The throne of grace is not set up that we may come and there vent our passions before God" (Wm. Gurnall). We are to spread our case before God, but leave it to His superior wisdom to prescribe how it shall be dealt with. There must be no dictating, nor can we "claim" anything from God, for we are beggars dependent upon His mere mercy. In all our praying we must add, "Nevertheless, not as I will, but as thou wilt."

But may not faith plead God's promises and expect an answer? Certainly; but it must be God's answer. Paul besought the Lord thrice to remove his thorn in the flesh; instead of doing so, the Lord gave him grace to endure it (2 Cor. 12). Many of God's promises are promiscuous rather than personal. He has promised His Church pastors, teachers and evangelists, yet many a local company of His saints has languished long without them. Some of God's promises are indefinite and general rather than absolute and universal; as, for example Ephesians 6:2, 3. God has not bound Himself to give in kind or specie, to grant the particular thing we ask for, even though we ask in faith. Moreover, He reserves to Himself the right to determine the fit time and season for bestowing His mercies. "Seek ye the Lord, all ye meek of the earth . . . it may be ye shall be hid in the day of the Lord's anger" (Zeph. 2:3). Just because it "may be" God's will to grant a certain temporal mercy unto me, it is my duty to cast myself upon Him and plead for it, yet with entire submission to His good pleasure for the performance of it.

7. We are profited from the Scriptures when prayer becomes a real and deep joy. Merely to "say our prayers each morning and evening is an irksome task, a duty to be performed which brings a sigh of relief when it is done. But really to come into the conscious presence of God, to behold the glorious light of His countenance, to commune with Him at the mercy seat, is a foretaste of the eternal bliss awaiting us in heaven. The one who is blessed with this experience says with the Psalmist, "It is good for me to draw near to God" (Ps. 73:28). Yes, good for the heart, for it is quietened; good for faith, for it is strengthened; good for the soul, for it is blessed. It is lack of this soul communion with God which is the root cause of our unanswered prayers: "Delight thyself also in the Lord; and he shall give thee the desires of thine heart" (Ps. 37:4).

What is it which, under the blessing of the Spirit, produces and promotes this joy in prayer? First, it is the heart's delight in God as the Object of prayer, and particularly the recognition and realization of God as our Father. Thus, when the disciples asked the Lord Jesus to teach them to pray, He said, "After this manner therefore pray ye: Our Father which art in heaven." And again, "God hath sent forth the Spirit of his Son into your hearts, crying, Abba [the Hebrew for "Father"], Father" (Gal. 4:6), which includes a filial, holy delight in God, such as children have in their parents in their most affectionate addresses to them. So again, in Ephesians 2:18, we are told, for the strengthening of faith and the comfort of our hearts, "For through him [Christ] we both have access by one Spirit unto the Father." What peace, what assurance, what freedom this gives to the soul: to know we are approaching our Father!

Second, joy in prayer is furthered by the heart's apprehension and the soul's sight of God as on the throne of grace — a sight or prospect, not by carnal imagination, but by spiritual illumination, for it is by faith that we "see him who is invisible" (Heb. 11:27); faith being the "evidence of things not seen" (Heb. 11:1), making its proper object evident and present unto them that believe. Such a sight of God upon such a "throne" cannot but thrill the soul. Therefore are we exhorted, "Let us therefore come boldly unto the throne of grace, that we may obtain mercy, and find grace to help in time of need" (Heb. 4:16).

Thirdly, and drawn from the last quoted scripture, freedom and delight in prayer are stimulated by the consciousness that God is, through Jesus Christ, willing and ready to dispense grace and mercy to suppliant sinners. There is no reluctance in Him which we have to overcome. He is more ready to give than we are to receive. So He is represented in Isaiah 30:18, "And therefore will the Lord wait, that He may be gracious unto you." Yes, He waits to be sought unto; waits for faith to lay hold of His readiness to bless. His ear is ever open to the cries of the righteous. Then "let us draw near with a true heart in full assurance of faith" (Heb. 10:22); "in everything by prayer and supplication with thanksgiving let your requests be made known unto God," and we shall find that peace which passes all understanding guarding our hearts and minds through Christ Jesus (Phil. 4:6, 7).

Arthur W. Pink

Chapter 5
The Scriptures and Good Works

The truth of God may well be likened to a narrow path skirted on either side by a dangerous and destructive precipice: in other words, it lies between two gulfs of error. The aptness of this figure may be seen in our proneness to sway from one extreme to another. Only the Holy Spirit's enabling can cause us to preserve the balance, failure to do which inevitably leads to a fall into error, for error is not so much the denial of truth as the perversion of truth, the pitting of one part of it against another.

The history of theology forcibly and solemnly illustrates this fact. One generation of men have rightly and earnestly contended for that aspect of truth which was most needed in their day. The next generation, instead of walking therein and moving forward, warred for it intellectually as the distinguishing mark of their party, and usually, in their defense of what was assaulted, have refused to listen to the balancing truth which often their opponents were insisting upon; the result being that they lost their sense of perspective and emphasized what they believed out of its scriptural proportions. Consequently, in the next generation, the true servant of God is called on almost to ignore what was so valuable in their eyes, and to emphasize that which they had, if not altogether denied, almost completely lost sight of.

It has been said that "Rays of light, whether they proceed from the sun, star, or candle, move in perfect straight lines; yet so inferior are our works to God's that the steadiest hand cannot draw a perfectly straight line; nor, with all his skill, has man ever been able to invent an instrument capable of doing a thing apparently so simple" (T. Guthrie, 1867). Be this so or not, certain it is that men, left to themselves, have ever found it impossible to keep the even line of truth between what appear to be conflicting doctrines:

such as the sovereignty of God and the responsibility of man; election by grace and the universal proclamation of the Gospel; the justifying faith of Paul and the justifying works of James. Only too often, where the absolute sovereignty of God has been insisted upon, it has been to the ignoring of man's accountability; and where unconditional election has been held fast, the unfettered preaching of the Gospel to the unsaved has been let slip. On the other hand, where human accountability has been upheld and an evangelical ministry been sustained, the sovereignty of God and the truth of election have generally been whittled down or completely ignored.

Many of our readers have witnessed examples which illustrate the truth of what has been said above, but few seem to realize that exactly the same difficulty is experienced when an attempt is made to show the precise relation between faith and good works. If, on the one hand, some have erred in attributing to good works a place which Scripture does not warrant, certain it is that, on the other hand, some have failed to give to good works the province which Scripture assigns them. If, on the one side, it be serious error to ascribe our justification before God to any performances of ours, on the other side they are equally guilty who deny that good works are necessary in order to our reaching heaven, and allow nothing more than that they are merely evidences or fruits of our justification. We are well aware that we are now (shall we say) treading on thin ice, and running a serious risk of ourselves being charged with heresy; nevertheless we deem it expedient to seek Divine aid in grappling with this difficulty, and then commit the issues thereof to God Himself.

In some quarters the claims of faith, though not wholly denied, have been disparaged because of a zeal to magnify good works. In other circles, reputed as orthodox (and they are what we now have chiefly in mind), only too rarely are good works assigned their proper place, and far too infrequently are professing Christians urged with apostolic earnestness to maintain them. No doubt this is due at times to a fear of undervaluing faith, and encouraging sinners in the fatal error of trusting to their own doings rather than to and in the righteousness of Christ. But no such apprehensions should hinder a preacher from declaring "all the counsel of God." If his theme be faith in Christ, as the Savior of the lost, let him fully set forth that truth without any modification, giving to this grace the place which the apostle gave it in his reply to the Philippian jailer (Acts 16:31). But if his subject be good works, let him be no less faithful in keeping back nothing which Scripture says thereon; let him not forget that Divine command, "Affirm constantly, that they which have believed in God might be careful to maintain good works" (Titus 3:8).

The last-quoted scripture is the most pertinent one for these days of looseness and laxity, of worthless profession, and empty boasting. This expression "good works" is found in the New Testament in the singular or plural number no less than thirty times; yet, from the rarity with which many preachers, who are esteemed sound in the faith, use, emphasize, and enlarge upon them, many of their hearers would conclude that those words occur but once or twice in all the Bible. Speaking to the Jews on another subject, the Lord said, "What. . . God hath joined together, let not man put asunder" (Mark 10:9). Now in Ephesians 2: 8-10, God has joined two most vital and blessed things together which ought never to be separated in our hearts and minds, yet they are most frequently parted in the modern pulpit. How many sermons are preached from the first two of these verses, which so clearly declare salvation to be by grace through faith and not of works. Yet how seldom are we reminded that the sentence which begins with grace and faith is only completed in verse 10, where we are told, "For we are His workmanship, created in Christ Jesus unto good works, which God hath before ordained that we should walk in them."

We began this series by pointing out that the Word of God may be taken up from various motives and read with different designs, but that 2 Timothy 3:16,17, makes known for what these Scriptures are really "profitable," namely for doctrine or teaching, for reproof, correction, instruction in righteousness, and all of these that "the man of God may be perfect, thoroughly furnished unto all good works." Having dwelt upon its teaching about God and Christ, its reproofs and corrections for sin, its instruction in connection with prayer, let us now consider how these furnish us unto "all good works." Here is another vital criterion by which an honest soul, with the help of the Holy Spirit, may ascertain whether or not his reading and study of the Word is really benefiting him.

1. We profit from the Word when we are thereby taught the true place of good works. "Many persons, in their eagerness to support orthodoxy as a system, speak of salvation by grace and faith

in such a manner as to undervalue holiness and a life devoted to God. But there is no ground for this in the Holy Scriptures. The same Gospel that declares salvation to be freely by the grace of God through faith in the blood of Christ, and asserts, in the strongest terms, that sinners are justified by the righteousness of the Savior imputed to them on their believing in Him, without any respect to works of law, also assures us, that without holiness no man shall see God; that believers are cleansed by the blood of atonement; that their hearts are purified by faith, which works by love, and overcomes the world; and that the grace that brings salvation to all men, teaches those who receive it, that denying ungodliness and worldly lusts, they should live soberly, righteously, and godly in this present world. Any fear that the doctrine of grace will suffer from the most strenuous inculcation of good works on a scriptural foundation, betrays an inadequate and greatly defective acquaintance with Divine truth, and any tampering with the Scriptures in order to silence their testimony in favor of the fruits of righteousness, as absolutely necessary in the Christian, is a perversion and forgery with respect to the Word of God" (Alexander Carson).

But what force (ask some) has this ordination or command of God unto good works, when, notwithstanding it, though we fail to apply ourselves diligently unto obedience, we shall nevertheless be justified by the imputation of Christ's righteousness, and so may be saved without them? Such a senseless objection proceeds from utter ignorance of the believer's present state and relation to God. To suppose that the hearts of the regenerate are not as much and as effectually influenced with the authority and commands of God unto obedience as if they were given in order unto their justification is to ignore what true faith is, and what are the arguments and motives whereby the minds of Christians are principally affected and constrained. Moreover, it is to lose sight of the inseparable connection which God has made between our justification and our sanctification: to suppose that one of these may exist without the other is to overthrow the whole Gospel. The apostle deals With this very objection in Romans 6:1-3.

2. We profit from the Word when we are thereby taught the absolute necessity of good works. If it be written that "without shedding of blood is no remission" (Heb. 9:22) and "without faith it is impossible to please him" (Heb. 11:6), the Scripture of Truth also declares, "Follow peace with all men, and holiness, without which

no man shall see the Lord" (Heb. 12:14). The life lived by the saints in heaven is but the completion and consummation of that life which, after regeneration, they live here on earth. The difference between the two is not one of kind, but of degree. "The path of the just is as the shining light, that shineth more and more unto the perfect day" (Prov. 4:18). If there has been no walking with God down here there will be no dwelling with God up there. If there has been no real communion with Him in time there will be none with Him in eternity. Death effects no vital change to the heart. True, at death the remainders of sin are forever left behind by the saint, but no new nature is then imparted. If then he did not hate sin and love holiness before death, he certainly will not do so afterwards.

No one really desires to go to hell, though there are few indeed who are willing to forsake that broad road which inevitably leads there. All would like to go to heaven, but professing Christians are really willing and determined to walk that narrow way which alone leads thereto? It is at this point that we may discern the precise place which good works have in connection with salvation. They do not merit it, yet they are inseparable from it. They do not procure a title to heaven, yet they are among the means which God has appointed for His people's getting there. In no sense are good works the procuring cause of eternal life, but they are part of the means (as are the Spirit's work within us and repentance, faith and obedience by us) conducing to it. God has appointed the way wherein we must walk in order to our arriving at the inheritance purchased for us by Christ. A life of daily obedience to God is that which alone gives actual admission to the enjoyment of what Christ has purchased for His people—admission now by faith, admission at death or His return in full actuality.

3. We profit from the Word when we are taught thereby the design of good works. This is clearly made known in Matthew 5:16: "Let your light so shine before men, that they may see your good works, and glorify your Father which is in heaven." It is worthy of our notice that this is the first occurrence of the expression, and, as is generally the case, the initial mention of a thing in Scripture intimates its subsequent scope and usage. Here we learn that the disciples of Christ are to authenticate their Christian profession by the silent but vocal testimony of their lives (for "light" makes no noise in its "shining"), that men may see (not hear boastings about) their good works, and this that their Father in heaven may

be glorified. Here, then, is their fundamental design: for the honor of God.

As the contents of Matthew 5:16 are so generally misunderstood and perverted we add a further thought thereon. Only too commonly the "good works" are confounded with the "light" itself, yet they are quite distinct, though inseparably connected. The "light" is our testimony for Christ but of what value is this unless the life itself exemplifies it? The "good works" are not for the directing of attention to ourselves, but to Him who has wrought them in us. They are to be of such a character and quality that even the ungodly will know they proceed from some higher source than fallen human nature. Supernatural fruit requires a supernatural root, and as this is recognized, the Husbandman is glorified thereby. Equally significant is the last reference to "good works" in Scripture: "Having your conversation honest among the Gentiles: that, whereas they speak against you as evildoers, they may by your good works, which they shall behold, glorify God in the day of visitation" (1 Pet. 2:12). Thus the first and final allusions emphasize their design: to glorify God because of His works through His people in this world.

4. We profit from the Word when we are taught thereby the true nature of good works. This is something concerning which the unregenerate are in entire ignorance. Judging merely from the external, estimating things only by human standards, they are quite incompetent to determine what works are good in God's esteem and what are not. Supposing that what men regard as good works God will approve of too, they remain in the darkness of their sin-blinded understandings; nor can any convince them of their error, till the Holy Spirit quickens them into newness of life, bringing them out of darkness into God's marvelous light. Then it will appear that only those are good works which are done in obedience to the will of God (Rom. 6:16), from a principle of love to Him (Heb. 10:24), in the name of Christ (Col. 3:17), and to the glory of God by Him (1 Cor. 10:31).

The true nature of "good works" Was perfectly exemplified by the Lord Jesus. All that He did was done in obedience to His Father. He "pleased not himself" (Rom. 15:3), but ever performed the bidding of the One who had sent Him (John 6:38). He could say, "I do always those things that please him" (John 8:29). There were no limits to Christ's subjection to the Father's will: He "became obedient unto death, even the death of the cross" (Phil. 2:8). So too all that He did proceeded from love to the Father and love to His neighbor. Love is the fulfilling of the Law; without love, compliance with the Law is naught but servile subjection, and that cannot be acceptable to Him who is Love. Proof that all Christ's obedience flowed from love is found in His words, "I delight to do thy will, O my God" (Ps. 40:8). So also all that Christ did had in view the glory of the Father: "Father, glorify thy name" (John 12:28) revealed the object constantly before Him.

5. We profit from the Word when we are taught thereby the true source of good works. Unregenerate men are capable of performing works which in a natural and civil sense, though not in the spiritual sense, are good. They may do those things which, externally, as to matter and substance of them, are good, such as reading the Bible, attending the ministry of the Word, giving alms to the poor; yet the mainspring of such actions, their lack of godly motive, renders them as filthy rags in the sight of the thrice holy One. The unregenerate have no power to perform works in a spiritual manner, and therefore it is written, "There is none that doeth good, no, not one" (Rom. 3:12). Nor are they able to: they are "not subject to the law of God, neither indeed can be" (Rom. 8:7). Hence, even the plowing of the wicked is sin (Prov. 21:4). Nor are believers able to think a good thought or perform a good work of themselves (2 Cor. 3:5): it is God who works in them "both to will and to do of his good pleasure" (Phil. 2:13).

When the Ethiopian can change his skin, and the leopard his spots, then may they also do good that are accustomed to do evil (Jer. 13:23). Men may as soon expect to gather grapes of thorns or figs of thistles, as good fruit to grow upon or good works to be performed by the unregenerate. We have first to be "created in Christ Jesus" (Eph. 2:10), have His Spirit put within us (Gal. 4:6), and His grace implanted in our hearts (Eph. 4: 7; I Cor. 15:10), before there is any capacity for good works. Even then we can do nothing apart from Christ (John 15:5). Often we have a will to do that which is good, yet how to perform it we know not (Rom. 7:18). This drives us to our knees, begging God to make us "perfect in every good work," working in us "that which is well-pleasing in his sight, through Jesus Christ" (Heb. 13:21). Thus we are emptied of self-sufficiency, and brought to realize that all our springs are in God (Ps. 87:7); and thus we discover that we can do all things through

Christ strengthening us (Phil. 4:13).

6. We profit from the Word when we are taught thereby the great importance of good works. Condensing as far as possible: "good works" are of great importance because by them God is glorified (Matt. 5:16), by them the mouths of those who speak against us are closed (1 Pet. 2:12), by them we evidence the genuineness of our profession of faith (James 2:13-17). It is highly expedient that we "adorn the doctrine of God our Savior in all things" (Titus 2:10). Nothing brings more honor to Christ than that those who bear His name are found living constantly (by His enablement) in a Christ-like way and spirit. It was not without reason that the same Spirit who caused the apostle to preface his statement concerning Christ's coming into this world to save sinners with "This is a faithful saying," etc., also moved him to write, "This is a faithful saying. . . that they which have believed in God might be careful to maintain good works" (Titus 3:8). May we indeed be "zealous of good works" (Titus 2:14).

7. We profit from the Word when we are taught thereby the true scope of good works. This is so comprehensive as to include the discharge of our duties in every relationship in which God has placed us. It is interesting and instructive to note the first "good work" (as so described) in Holy Writ, namely, the anointing of the Savior by Mary of Bethany (Matt. 26:10; Mark 14:6). Indifferent alike to the blame or praise of men, with eyes only for the "chiefest among ten thousand," she lavished upon Him her precious ointment. Another woman, Dorcas (Acts 9:36), is also mentioned as "full of good works"; after worship comes service, glorifying God among men and benefiting others.

"That ye might walk worthy of the Lord unto all pleasing, being fruitful in every good work" (Col. 1:10). The bringing up (not "dragging" up!) of children, lodging (spiritual) strangers, washing the saints" feet (ministering to their temporal comforts) and relieving the afflicted (1 Tim. 5:10) are spoken of as "good works." Unless our reading and study of the Scriptures is making us better soldiers of Jesus Christ, better citizens of the country in which we sojourn, better members of our earthly homes (kinder, gentler, more unselfish), "thoroughly furnished unto all good works," it is profiting us little or nothing.

Arthur W. Pink

Chapter 6
The Scriptures and Obedience

All professing Christians are agreed, in theory at least, that it is the bounden duty of those who bear His name to honor and glorify Christ in this world. But as to how this is to be done, as to what He requires from us to this end, there is wide difference of opinion. Many suppose that honoring Christ simply means to join some "church," take part in and support its various activities. Others think that honoring Christ means to speak of Him to others and be diligently engaged in "personal work." Others seem to imagine that honoring Christ signifies little more than making liberal financial contributions to His cause. Few indeed realize that Christ is honored only as we live holily unto Him, and that, by walking in subjection to His revealed will. Few indeed really believe that word, "Behold, to obey is better than sacrifice, and to hearken than the fat of rams" (1 Sam. 15:22).

We are not Christians at all unless we have fully surrendered to and "received Christ Jesus the Lord" (Col. 2:6). We would plead with you to ponder that statement diligently. Satan is deceiving many today by leading them to suppose that they are savingly trusting in "the finished work" of Christ while their hearts remain unchanged and self still rules their lives. Listen to God's Word: "Salvation is far from the wicked; for they seek not thy statutes" (Ps. 119:155). Do you really seek His statutes"? Do you diligently search His Word to discover what He has commanded? "He that saith, I know Him, and keepeth not his commandments, is a liar, and the truth is not in him" (1 John 2:4). What could be plainer than that?

"And why call ye me, Lord, Lord, and do not the things which I say?" (Luke 6:46). Obedience to the Lord in life, not merely glowing words from the lips, is what Christ requires. What a searching and solemn word is that in James 1:22: "Be ye doers of the word, and not hearers only, deceiving your own selves"! There are many "hearers" of the Word, regular hearers, reverent hearers, interested hearers; but alas, what they hear is not incorporated into the life: it does not regulate their way. And God says that they who are not doers of the Word are deceiving their own selves!

Alas, how many such there are in Christendom today! They are not downright hypocrites, but deluded. They suppose that because they are so clear upon salvation by grace alone they are saved. They suppose that because they sit under the ministry of a man who has "made the Bible a new book" to them they have grown in grace. They suppose that because their store of biblical knowledge has increased they are more spiritual. They suppose that the mere listening to a servant of God or reading his writings is feeding on the Word. Not so! We "feed" on the Word only when we personally appropriate, masticate and assimilate into our lives what we hear or read. Where there is not an increasing conformity of heart and life to God's Word, then increased knowledge will only bring increased condemnation. "And that servant, which knew his lord's will, and prepared not himself, neither did according to his will, shall be beaten with many stripes" (Luke 12:47).

"Ever learning, and never able to come to the knowledge of the truth" (2 Tim 3:7). This is one of the prominent characteristics of the "perilous times" in which we are now living. People hear one preacher after another, attend this conference and that conference, read book after book on biblical subjects, and yet never attain unto a vital and practical acquaintance with the truth, so as to have an impression of its power and efficacy on the soul. There is such a thing as spiritual dropsy, and multitudes are suffering from it. The more they hear, the more they want to hear: they drink in sermons and addresses with avidity, but their lives are unchanged. They are puffed up with their knowledge, not humbled into the dust before God. The faith of God's elect is "the acknowledging [in the life] of the truth which is after godliness" (Titus 1:1), but to this the vast majority are total strangers.

God has given us His Word not only with the design of instructing us, but for the purpose of directing us: to make known what He requires us to do. The first thing we need is a clear and distinct knowledge of our duty; and the first thing God demands of us is a conscientious practice of it, corresponding to our knowledge.

"What doth the Lord require of thee, but to do justly, and to love mercy, and to walk humbly with thy God?" (Micah 6:8). "Let us hear the conclusion of the whole matter: Fear God, and keep his commandments: for this is the whole duty of man (Eccles. 12:13). The Lord Jesus affirmed the same thing when He said, "Ye are my friends, if ye do whatsoever I command you" (John 15:14).

1. A man profits from the Word as he discovers God's demands upon him; His undeviating demands, for He changes not. It is a great and grievous mistake to suppose that in this present dispensation God has lowered His demands, for that would necessarily imply that His previous demand was a harsh and unrighteous one. Not so! "The law is holy, and the commandment holy, and just, and good" (Rom. 7:12). The sum of God's demands is, "Thou shalt love the Lord thy God with all thine heart, and with all thy soul, and with all thy might" (Deut. 6:5); and the Lord Jesus repeated it in Matthew 22:37. The apostle Paul enforced the same when he wrote, "If any man love not the Lord Jesus Christ let him be Anathema" (1 Cor. 16:22).

2. A man profits from the Word when he discovers how entirely and how sinfully he has failed to meet God's demands. And let us point out for the benefit of any who may take issue with the last paragraph that no man can see what a sinner he is, how infinitely short he has fallen of measuring up to God's standard, until he has a clear sight of the exalted demands of God upon him! Just in proportion as preachers lower God's standard of what He requires from every human being, to that extent will their hearers obtain an inadequate and faulty conception of their sinfulness, and the less will they perceive their need of an almighty Savior. But once a soul really perceives what are God's demands upon him, and how completely and constantly he has failed to render Him His due, then does he recognize what a desperate situation he is in. The law must be preached before any are ready for the Gospel.

3. A man profits from the Word when he is taught therefrom that God, in His infinite grace, has fully provided for His people's meeting His own demands. At this point, too, much present-day preaching is seriously defective. There is being given forth what may loosely be termed a "half Gospel," but which in reality is virtually a denial of the true Gospel. Christ is brought in, yet only as a sort of make-weight. That Christ has vicariously met every demand of God upon all who believe upon Him is blessedly true, yet

it is only a part of the truth. The Lord Jesus has not only vicariously satisfied for His people the requirements of God's righteousness, but He has also secured that they shall personally satisfy them too. Christ has procured the Holy Spirit to make good in them what the Redeemer wrought for them.

The grand and glorious miracle of salvation is that the saved are regenerated. A transforming work is wrought within them. Their understandings are illuminated, their hearts are changed, their wills are renewed. They are made "new creatures in Christ Jesus" (2 Cor. 5:17). God refers to this miracle of grace thus: "I will put my laws into their mind, and write them in their hearts" (Heb. 8:10). The heart is now inclined to God's law: a disposition has been communicated to it which answers to its demands; there is a sincere desire to perform it. And thus the quickened soul is able to say, "When thou saidst, Seek ye my face; my heart said unto thee, thy face, Lord, will I seek" (Ps. 27:8).

Christ not only rendered a perfect obedience unto the Law for the justification of His believing people, but He also merited for them those supplies of His Spirit which were essential unto their sanctification, and which alone could transform carnal creatures and enable them to render acceptable obedience unto God. Though Christ died for the "ungodly" (Rom. 5:6), though He finds them ungodly (Rom. 4:5) when He justifies them, yet He does not leave them in that abominable state. On the contrary, He effectually teaches them by His Spirit to deny ungodliness and worldly lusts (Titus 2:12). Just as weight cannot be separated from a stone, or heat from a fire, so cannot justification from sanctification.

When God really pardons a sinner in the court of his Conscience, under the sense of that amazing grace the heart is purified, the life is rectified, and the whole man is sanctified. Christ "gave himself for us, that he might redeem us from all iniquity, and purify unto himself a peculiar people [not "careless about" but], zealous of good works" (Titus 2:14). Just as a substance and its properties, causes and their necessary effects are inseparably connected, so are a saving faith and conscientious obedience unto God. Hence we read of "the obedience of faith" (Rom. 16:26).

Said the Lord Jesus, "He that hath my commandments, and keepeth them, he it is that loveth me" (John 14:21). Not in the Old Testament, the Gospels or the Epistles does God own anyone as a lover of Him save the one who keeps His commandments. Love is something more than sentiment or emotion; it is a principle of action, and it expresses itself in something more than honeyed expressions, namely, by deeds which please the object loved. "For this is the love of God, that we keep his commandments" (1 John 5:3). Oh, my reader, you are deceiving yourself if you think you love God and yet have no deep desire and make no real effort to walk obediently before Him.

But what is obedience to God? It is far more than a mechanical performance of certain duties. I may have been brought up by Christian parents, and under them acquired certain moral habits, and yet my abstaining from taking the Lord's name in vain, and being guiltless of stealing, may be no obedience to the third and eighth commandments. Again, obedience to God is far more than conforming to the conduct of His people. I may board in a home where the Sabbath is strictly observed, and out of respect for them, or because I think it is a good and wise course to rest one day in seven, I may refrain from all unnecessary labor on that day, and yet not keep the fourth commandment at all! Obedience is not only subjection to an external law, but it is the surrendering of my will to the authority of another. Thus, obedience to God is the heart's recognition of His lordship: of His right to command, and my duty to comply. It is the complete subjection of the soul to the blessed yoke of Christ.

That obedience which God requires can proceed only from a heart which loves Him. "Whatsoever ye do, do it heartily, as to the Lord" (Col. 3:23). That obedience which springs from a dread of punishment is servile. That obedience which is performed in order to procure favors from God is selfish and carnal. But spiritual and acceptable obedience is cheerfully given: it is the heart's free response to and gratitude for the unmerited regard and love of God for us.

4. We profit from the Word when we not only see it is our bounden duty to obey God, but when there is wrought in us a love for His commandments. The "blessed" man is the one whose "delight is in the law of the Lord" (Ps. 1:2).And again we read, "Blessed is the man that feareth the Lord, that delighteth greatly in his commandments" (Ps. 112:1). It affords a real test for our hearts to face honestly the questions, Do I really value His "commandments" as much as I do His promises? Ought I not to do so? Assuredly, for the one proceeds as truly from His love as does the other. The

heart's compliance with the voice of Christ is the foundation for all practical holiness.

Here again we would earnestly and lovingly beg the reader to attend closely to this detail. Any man who supposes that he is saved and yet has no genuine love for God's commandment is deceiving himself. Said the Psalmist, "O how love I thy law!" (Ps. 119:97). And again, "Therefore I love thy commandments above gold; yea, above fine gold" (Ps. 119:127). Should someone object that that was under the Old Testament, we ask, Do you intimate that the Holy Spirit produces a lesser change in the hearts of those whom He now regenerates than He did of old? But a New Testament saint also placed on record, "I delight in the law of God after the inward man" (Rom. 7:22). And, my reader, unless your heart delights in the "law of God" there is something radically wrong with you; yea, it is greatly to be feared that you are spiritually dead.

5. A man profits from the Word when his heart and will are yielded to all God's commandments. Partial obedience is no obedience at all. A holy mind declines whatsoever God forbids, and chooses to practice all He requires, without any exception. If our minds submit not unto God in all His commandments, we submit not to His authority in anything He enjoins. If we do not approve of our duty in its full extent, we are greatly mistaken if we imagine that we have any liking unto any part of it. A person who has no principle of holiness in him may yet be disinclined to many vices and be pleased to practice many virtues, as he perceives the former are unfit actions and the latter are, in themselves, comely actions, but his disapprobation of vice and approbation of virtue do not arise from any disposition to submit to the will of God.

True spiritual obedience is impartial. A renewed heart does not pick and choose from God's commandments: the man who does so is not performing God's will, but his own. Make no mistake upon this point; if we do not sincerely desire to please God in all things, then we do not truly wish to do so in anything. Self must be denied; not merely some of the things which may be craved, but self itself! A willful allowance of any known sin breaks the whole law (James 2:10, 11). "Then shall I not be ashamed, when I have respect unto all thy commandments" (Ps. 119:6). Said the Lord Jesus, "Ye are my friends, if ye do whatsoever I command you" (John 15:14): if I am not His friend, then I must be His enemy, for there is no other alternative-see Luke 19:27.

6. We profit from the Word when the soul is moved to pray earnestly for enabling grace. In regeneration the Holy Spirit communicates a nature which is fitted for obedience according to the Word. The heart has been won by God. There is now a deep and sincere desire to please Him. But the new nature possesses no inherent power, and the old nature or "flesh" strives against it, and the Devil opposes. Thus, the Christian exclaims, "To will is present with me; but how to perform that which is good I find not" (Rom. 7:18). This does not mean that he is the slave of sin, as he was before conversion; but it means that he finds not how fully to realize his spiritual aspirations. Therefore does he pray, "Make me to go in the path of Thy commandments; for therein do I delight" (Ps. 119:35). And again, "Order my steps in Thy word, and let not any iniquity have dominion over me" (Ps. 119:133).

Here we would reply to a question which the above statements have probably raised in many minds: Are you affirming that God requires perfect obedience from us in this life? We answer, Yes! God will not set any lower standard before us than that (see 1 Pet. 1:15). Then does the real Christian measure up to that standard? Yes and no! Yes, in his heart, and it is at the heart that God looks (I Sam. 16:7). In his heart every regenerated person has a real love for God's commandments, and genuinely desires to keep all of them completely. It is in this sense, and this alone, that the Christian is experimentally "perfect." The word "perfect," both in the Old Testament (Job 1:1, and Ps. 37:37) and in the New Testament (Phil. 3:15), means "upright", "sincere", in contrast with "hypocritical".

"Lord, thou hast heard the desire of the humble" (Ps. 10:17). The "desires" of the saint are the language of his soul, and the promise is, "He will fulfill the desire of them that fear him" (Ps. 145:19). The Christian's desire is to obey God in all things, to be completely conformed to the image of Christ. But this will only be realized in the resurrection. Meanwhile, God for Christ's sake graciously accepts the will for the deed (1 Pet. 2:5). He knows our hearts and see in His child a genuine love for and a sincere desire to keep all His commandments, and He accepts the fervent longing and cordial endeavor in lieu of an exact performance (2 Cor. 8:12). But let none who are living in willful disobedience draw false peace and pervert to their own destruction what has just been said for the comfort of those who are heartily desirous of seeking to please God in all the details of their lives.

If any ask, How am I to know that my "desires" are really those of a regenerate soul? we answer, Saving grace is the communication to the heart of an habitual disposition unto holy acts. The "desires" of the reader are to be tested thus: Are they constant and continuous, or only by fits and starts? Are they earnest and serious, so that you really hunger and thirst after righteousness" (Matt. 5:6) and pant "after God" (Ps. 42:1)? Are they operative and efficacious? Many desire to escape from hell, yet their desires are not sufficiently strong to bring them to hate and turn from that which must inevitably bring them to hell, namely, willful sinning against God. Many desire to go to heaven, but not so that they enter upon and follow that "narrow way" which alone leads there. True spiritual desires use the means of grace and spare no pains to realize them, and continue prayerfully pressing forward unto the mark set before them.

7. We profit from the Word when we are, even now, enjoying the reward of obedience. "Godliness is profitable unto all things" (1 Tim. 4:8). By obedience we purify our souls (1 Pet. 1:21). By obedience we obtain the ear of God (1 John 3:22), just as disobedience is a barrier to our prayers (Isa. 59:2; Jer. 5:25). By obedience we obtain precious and intimate manifestations of Christ unto the soul (John 14:21). As we tread the path of wisdom (complete subjection to God) we discover that "her ways are ways of pleasantness, and all her paths are peace" (Prov. 3:17). "His commandments are not grievous" (1 John 5:3), and "in keeping of them there is great reward" (Ps. 19:11).

Arthur W. Pink

Chapter 7
The Scriptures and the World

Not a little is written to the Christian in the New Testament about "the world" and his attitude towards it. Its real nature is plainly defined, and the believer is solemnly warned against it. God's holy Word is a light from heaven, shining here "in a dark place" (2 Pet. 1:19). Its Divine rays exhibit things in their true colors, penetrating and exposing the false veneer and glamour by which many objects are cloaked. That world upon which so much labor is bestowed and money spent, and which is so highly extolled and admired by its blinded dupes, is declared to be "the enemy of God"; therefore are His children forbidden to be "conformed" to it and to have their affections set upon it.

The present phase of our subject is by no means the least important of those that we have set out to consider, and the serious reader will do well to seek Divine grace to measure himself or herself by it. One of the exhortations which God has addressed to His children runs, "As newborn babes, desire the sincere milk of the word, that ye may grow thereby" (1 Pet. 2:2), and it behooves each one of them honestly and diligently to examine himself so as to discover whether or not this be the case with him. Nor are we to be content with an increase of mere head-knowledge of Scripture: what we need to be most concerned about is our practical growth, our experimental conformity to the image of Christ. And one point at which we may test ourselves is, Does my reading and study of God's Word make me less worldly?

1. We profit from the Word when our eyes are opened to discern the true character of the world. One of the poets wrote, "God's in His heaven—all's right with the world". From one standpoint that is blessedly true, but from another it is radically wrong, for "the whole world lieth in wickedness" (1 John 5:19). But it is only as the heart is supernaturally enlightened by the Holy Spirit that we are enabled to perceive that that which is highly esteemed among

men is really "abomination in the sight of God" (Luke 16:15). It is much to be thankful for when the soul is able to see that the "world" is a gigantic fraud, a hollow bauble, a vile thing, which must one day be burned up.

Before we go further, let us define that "world" which the Christian is forbidden to love. There are few words found upon the pages of Holy Writ used with a greater variety of meanings than this one. Yet careful attention to the context will usually determine its scope. The "world" is a system or order of things, complete in itself. No foreign element is suffered to intrude, or if it does it is speedily accommodated or assimilated to itself. The "world" is fallen human nature acting itself out in the human family, fashioning the framework of human society in accord with its own tendencies. It is the organized kingdom of the "carnal mind" which is "enmity against God" and which is "not subject to the law of God, neither indeed can be" (Rom. 8:7). Wherever the "carnal mind" is, there is "the world"; so that worldliness is the world without God.

2. We profit from the Word when we learn that the world is an enemy to be resisted and overcome. The Christian is bidden to "fight the good fight of faith" (1 Tim. 6:12), which implies that there are foes to be met and vanquished. As there is the Holy Trinity—the Father, the Son, and the Holy Spirit—so also is there an evil trinity—the flesh, the world, and the Devil. The child of God is called to engage in a mortal combat with them; "mortal", we say, for either they will destroy him or he will get the victory over them. Settle it, then, in your mind, my reader, that the world is a deadly enemy, and if you do not vanquish it in your heart then you are no child of God, for it is written "Whatsoever is born of God overcometh the world" (1 John 5:4).

Out of many, the following reasons may be given as to why the world must be "overcome." First, all its alluring objects tend to divert the attention and alienate the affections of the soul from God. Necessarily so, for it is the tendency of things seen to turn the heart away from things unseen. Second, the spirit of the world is diametrically opposed to the Spirit of Christ; therefore did the apostle write, "Now we have received, not the spirit of the world, but the Spirit which is of God" (1 Cor. 2:12). The Son of God came into the world, but "the world knew him not" (John 1:10); therefore did its "princes" and rulers crucify Him (1 Cor. 2:8). Third, its concerns and cares are hostile to a devout and heavenly life.

Christians, like the rest of mankind, are required by God to labor six days in the week; but while so employed they need to be constantly on their guard, lest covetous interests govern them rather than the performance of duty.

"This is the victory that overcometh the world, even our faith" (1 John 5:4). Naught but a God-given faith can overcome the world. But as the heart is occupied with invisible yet eternal realities, it is delivered from the corrupting influence of worldly objects. The eyes of faith discern the things of sense in their real colors, and see that they are empty and vain, and not worthy to be compared with the great and glorious objects of eternity. A felt sense of the perfections and presence of God makes the world appear less than nothing. When the Christian views the Divine Redeemer dying for his sins, living to intercede for his perseverance, reigning and overruling things for his final salvation, he exclaims, "There is none upon earth that I desire beside thee."

And how is it with you as you read these lines? You may cordially assent to what has just been said in the last paragraph, but how is it with you actually? Do the things which are so highly valued by the unregenerate charm and enthral you? Take away from the worldling those things in which he delights, and he is wretched: is this so with you? Or, are your present joy and satisfaction found in objects which can never be taken from you? Treat not these questions lightly, we beseech you, but ponder them seriously in the presence of God. The honest answer to them will be an index to the real state of your soul, and will indicate whether or not you are deceived in supposing yourself to be "a new creature in Christ Jesus."

3. We profit from the Word when we learn that Christ died to deliver us from "this present evil world" (Gal. 1:4). The Son of God came here, not only to "fulfill" the requirements of the law (Matt. 5:17), to "destroy the works of the devil" (1 John 3:8), to deliver us "from the wrath to come" (1 Thess. 1:10), to save us from our sins (Matt. 1:21), but also to free us from the bondage of this world, to deliver the soul from its enthralling influence. This was foreshadowed of old in God's dealings with Israel. They were slaves in Egypt, and "Egypt" is a figure of the world. They were in cruel bondage, spending their time in making bricks for Pharaoh. They were unable to free themselves. But Jehovah, by His mighty power, emancipated them, and brought them forth out of the "iron

furnace." Thus does Christ with His own. He breaks the power of the world over their hearts. He makes them independent of it, that they neither court its favors nor fear its frowns.

Christ gave Himself a sacrifice for the sins of His people that, in consequence thereof, they might be delivered from the damning power and governing influence of all that is evil in this present world: from Satan, who is its prince; from the lusts which predominate in it; from the vain conversation of the men who belong to it. And the Holy Spirit indwelling the saints co-operates with Christ in this blessed work. He turns their thoughts and affections away from earthly things to heavenly. By the working of His power, lie frees them from the demoralizing influence which surrounds them, and conforms them to the heavenly standard. And as the Christian grows in grace he recognizes this, and acts accordingly. He seeks yet fuller deliverance from this "present evil world," and begs God to free him from it completely. That which once charmed him now nauseates. He longs for the time when he shall be taken out of this scene where his blessed Lord is so grievously dishonored.

4. We profit from the Word when our hearts are weaned from it. "Love not the world, neither the things that are in the world" (1 John 2:15). "What the stumbling-block is to the traveler in the way, the weight to the runner, the lime twigs to the bird in its flight, so is the love of the world to a Christian in his course—either wholly diverting him from, greatly enticing him in, or forcibly turning him out of it" (Nathaniel Hardy, 1660). The truth is that until the heart is purged from this corruption the ear will be deaf to Divine instruction. Not until we are lifted above the things of time and sense can we be subdued unto obedience to God. Heavenly truth glides off a carnal mind as water from a spherical body.

The world has turned its back upon Christ, and though His name is professed in many places, yet will it have nothing to do with Him. All the desires and designs of worldlings are for the gratification of self. Let their aims and pursuits be as varied as they may, self being supreme, everything is subordinated to the pleasing of self. Now Christians are in the world, and cannot get out of it; they have to live their Lord's appointed time in it. While here they have to earn their living, support their families, and attend to their worldly business. But they are forbidden to love the world, as though it could make them happy. Their "treasure" and "portion" are to be found elsewhere.

The world appeals to every instinct of fallen man. It contains a thousand objects to charm him: they attract his attention, the attention creates a desire for and love of them, and insensibly yet surely they make deeper and deeper impressions on his heart. It has the same fatal influence on all classes. But attractive and appealing as its varied objects may be, all the pursuits and pleasures of the world are designed and adapted to promote the happiness of this life only therefore, "What shall it profit a man if he should gain the whole world, and lose his own soul?" The Christian is taught by the Spirit, and through His presenting of Christ to the soul his thoughts are diverted from the world. Just as a little child will readily drop a dirty object when something more pleasing is offered to it, so the heart which is in communion with God will say, "I count all things but loss for the excellency of the knowledge of Christ Jesus my Lord... and do count them but dung, that I may win Christ" (Phil. 3:8).

5. We profit from the Word when we walk in separation from the world. "Know ye not that the friendship of the world is enmity with God? whosoever will be a friend of the world is the enemy of God" (James 4:4). Such a verse as this ought to search every one of us through and through, and make us tremble. How can I fraternize with or seek my pleasure in that which condemned the Son of God? If I do, that at once identifies me with His enemies. Oh, my reader, make no mistake upon this point. It is written, "If any man love the world, the love of the Father is not in him" (1 John 2:15).

Of old it was said of the people of God that they "shall dwell alone, and shall not be reckoned among the nations" (Num. 23:9). Surely the disparity of character and conduct, the desires and pursuits, which distinguish the regenerate from the unregenerate must separate the one from the other. We who profess to have our citizenship in another world, to be guided by another Spirit, to be directed by another rule, and to be journeying to another country, cannot go arm in arm with those who despise all such things! Then let everything in and about us exhibit the character of Christian pilgrims. May we indeed be "men wondered at" (Zech. 3:8) because "not conformed to this world" (Rom. 12:2).

6. We profit from the Word when we evoke the hatred of the world. What pains are taken in the world to save appearances and keep up a seemly and good state! Its conventionalities and civili-

ties, its courtesies and charities, are so many contrivances to give an air of respectability to it. So too its churches and cathedrals, its priests and prelates, are needed to gloss over the corruption which seethes beneath the surface. And to make good weight "Christianity" is added, and the holy name of Christ is taken upon the lips by thousands who have never taken His "yoke" upon them. Of them God says, "This people draweth nigh unto me with their mouth and honoreth me with their lips; but their heart is far from me" (Matt. 15:8).

And what is to be the attitude of all real Christians toward such? The answer of Scripture is plain: "From such turn away" (2 Tim. 3:5), "Come out from among them, and be ye separate, saith the Lord" (2 Cor. 6:17). And what will follow when this Divine command is obeyed? Why, then we shall prove the truth of those words of Christ: "If ye were of the world, the world would love his own: but because ye are not of the world, but I have chosen you out of the world, therefore the world hateth you (John 15:19). Which "world" is specifically in view here? Let the previous verse answer: "If the world hate you, ye know that it hated me before it hated you."

What "world" hated Christ and hounded Him to death? The religious world, those who pretended to be most zealous for God's glory. So it is now. Let the Christian turn his back upon a Christ—dishonoring Christendom, and his fiercest foes and most relentless and unscrupulous enemies will be those who claim to be Christians themselves! But "Blessed are ye, when men shall revile you, and persecute you ... for my sake. Rejoice, and be exceeding glad" (Matt. 5:11,12). Ah, my brother, it is a healthy sign, a sure mark that you are profiting from the Word, when the religious world hates you. But if, on the other hand, you still have a "good standing" in the "churches" or "assemblies" there is grave reason to fear that you love the praise of men more than that of God!

7. We profit from the Word when we are elevated above the world. First, above its customs and fashions. The worldling is a slave to the prevailing habits and styles of the day. Not so the one who is walking with God: his chief concern is to be "conformed to the image of his Son." Second, above its cares and sorrows: of old it was said of the saints that they took joyfully the spoiling of their goods, knowing that they had "in heaven a better and an enduring substance" (Heb. 10:34). Third, above its temptations: what attraction has the glare and glitter of the world for those who are

"delighting themselves in the Lord?" None whatever! Fourth, above its opinions and approvals. Have you learned to be independent of and defy the world? If your whole heart is set upon pleasing God, you will be quite unconcerned about the frowns of the godless.

Now, my reader, do you really wish to measure yourself by the contents of this chapter? Then seek honest answers to the following questions. First, what are the objects before your mind in times of recreation? What do your thoughts most run upon? Second, what are the objects of your choice? When you have to decide how to spend an evening or the Sabbath afternoon, what do you select? Third, which occasions you the most sorrow, the loss of earthly things, or lack of communion with God? Which causes greater grief (or chagrin), the spoiling of your plans, or the coldness of your heart to Christ? Fourth, what is your favorite topic of conversation? Do you hanker after the news of the day, or to meet with those who talk of the "altogether lovely" One? Fifth, do your "good intentions" materialize, or are they nothing but empty dreams? Are you spending more or less time than formerly on your knees? Is the Word sweeter to your taste, or has your soul lost its relish for it?

Chapter 8
The Scriptures and the Promises

The Divine promises make known the good pleasure of God's will to His people, to bestow upon them the riches of His grace. They are the outward testimonies of His heart, who from all eternity loves them and foreappointed all things for them and concerning them. In the person and work of His Son, God has made an all-sufficient provision for their complete salvation, both for time and for eternity. To the intent that they might have a true, clear and spiritual knowledge of the same, it has pleased the Lord to set it before them in the exceeding great and precious promises which are scattered up and down in the Scriptures as so many stars in the glorious firmament of grace; by which they may be assured of the will of God in Christ Jesus concerning them, and take sanctuary in Him accordingly, and through this medium have real communion with Him in His grace and mercy at all times, no matter what their case or circumstances may be.

The Divine promises are so many declarations to bestow some good or remove some ill. As such they are a most blessed making known and manifesting of God's love to His people. There are three steps in connection with God's love: first, His inward purpose to exercise it; the last, the real execution of that purpose; but in between there is the gracious making known of that purpose to the beneficiaries not only show His love fully to them in due time, but in the interim He will have us informed of His benevolent designs, that we may sweetly rest in His love, and stretch ourselves comfortably upon His sure promises. There we are able to say, "How precious also are thy thoughts unto me, 0 God! how great is the sum of them" (Ps. 139:17).

In 2 Peter 1:4, the Divine promises are spoken of as "exceeding great and precious." As Spurgeon pointed out, "greatness and preciousness seldom go together, but in this instance they are united in an exceeding degree". When Jehovah is pleased to open His mouth and reveal His heart He does so in a manner worthy of Himself, in words of superlative power and richness. To quote again the beloved London pastor: "They come from a great God, they come to great sinners, they work for us great results, and deal with great matters." While the natural intellect is capable of perceiving much of their greatness, only the renewed heart can taste their ineffable preciousness, and say with David, "How sweet are thy words unto my taste! yea, sweeter then honey to my mouth" (Ps. 119:103).

1. We profit from the Word when we perceive to whom the promises belong. They are available Only to those who are in Christ. "For all the promises of God in him [the Lord Jesus] are yea, and in him Amen" (2 Cor. I :20). There can be no intercourse between the thrice holy God and sinful creatures except through a Mediator who has satisfied Him on their behalf. Therefore must that Mediator receive from God all good for His people, and they must have it at second hand through Him. A sinner might just as well petition a tree as call upon God for mercy while he despises and rejects Christ.

Both the promises and the things promised are made over to the Lord Jesus and conveyed unto the saints from Him. "This is the [chief and grandest] promise that he hath promised us, even eternal life" (1 John 2:25), and as the same epistle tells us, "This life is in his Son" (5:11). This being so, what good can they who are not yet in Christ have by the promises? None at all. A man out of Christ is out of the favor of God, yea, he is under His wrath; the Divine threatenings and not the promises are his portion. Solemn, solemn consideration is it that those who are "without Christ" are "aliens from the commonwealth of Israel, and strangers from the covenants of promise, having no hope, and without God in the world" (Eph. 2:12). Only "the children of God" are "the children of the promise" (Rom. 9:8). Make sure, my reader, that you are one of them.

How terrible, then, is the blindness and how great is the sin of those preachers who indiscriminately apply the Divine promises to the saved and unsaved alike! They are not only taking "the children's bread" and casting it to the "dogs," but they are "handling the word of God deceitfully" (2 Cor. 4:2), and beguiling immortal souls. And they who listen to and heed them are little less guilty, for God holds all responsible to search the Scriptures for themselves, and test whatever they read or hear by that unerring standard. If they are too lazy to do so, and prefer blindly to follow their blind guides, then their blood is on their own heads. Truth has to be "bought" (Prov. 23:23), and those who are unwilling to pay the price must go without it.

2. We profit from the Word when we labor to make the promises of God our own. To do this we must first take the trouble to become really acquainted with them. It is surprising how many promises there are in Scripture which the saints know nothing about, the more so seeing that they are the peculiar treasure of believers, the substance of faith's heritage lying in them. True, Christians are already the recipients of wondrous blessings, yet the capital of their wealth, the bulk of their estate, is only prospective. They have already received an "earnest," but the better part of what Christ has purchased for them lies yet in the promise of God. How diligent, then, should they be in studying His testamentary will, familiarizing themselves with the good things which the Spirit "hath revealed" (1 Cor. 2:10), and seeking to take an inventory of their spiritual treasures!

Not only must I search the Scriptures to find out what has been made over to me by the everlasting covenant, but I need also to meditate upon the promises, to turn them over and over in my mind, and cry unto the Lord for spiritual understanding of them. The bee would not extract honey from the flowers as long as he only gazed upon them. Nor will the Christian derive any real comfort and strength from the Divine promises until his faith lays hold of and penetrates to the heart of them. God has given no assurance that the dilatory shall be fed, but He has declared, "the soul of the diligent shall be made fat" (Prov. 13:4). Therefore did Christ say, "Labor not for the meat which perisheth, but for that meat which endureth unto everlasting life" (John 6:27). It is only as the promises are stored up in our minds that the Spirit brings them to remembrance at those seasons of fainting when we most need them.

3. We profit from the Word when we recognize the blessed scope of God's promises. "A sort of affectation prevents some Christians from seeking religion, as if its sphere lay among the commonplac-

es of daily life. It is to them transcendental and dreamy; rather a creation of pious fiction than a matter of fact. They believe in God, after a fashion, for things spiritual, and for the life which is to be; but they totally forget that true godliness hath the promise of the life which now is, as well as that which is to come. To them it would seem almost profanation to pray about the small matters of which daily life is made up. Perhaps they will be startled if I venture to suggest that this should make them question the reality of their faith. If it cannot bring them help in the little troubles of life, will it support them in the greater trials of death?" (C. H. Spurgeon).

"Godliness is profitable unto all things, having promise of the life that now is, and of that which is to come" (1 Tim. 4:8). Reader, do you really believe this, that the promises of God cover every aspect and particular of your daily life? Or have the "Dispensationalists" deluded you into supposing that the Old Testament belongs only to fleshly Jews, and that "our promises" respect spiritual and not material blessings? How many a Christian has derived comfort from "I will never leave thee, nor forsake thee" (Heb. 13:5); well, that is a quotation from Joshua 1:5! So, too, 2 Corinthians 7:1 speaks of "having these promises," yet one of them, referred to in 6:18, is taken from the book of Leviticus!

Perhaps someone asks, "But where am I to draw the line? Which of the Old Testament promises rightfully belong to me?" We answer that Psalm 84:11 declares, "The Lord will give grace and glory: no good thing will He withhold from them that walk uprightly". If you are really walking "uprightly" you are entitled to appropriate that blessed promise and count upon the Lord giving you whatever "good thing" is truly required by you. "My God shall supply all your need" (Phil. 4:19). If then there is a promise anywhere in His Word which just fits your present case and situation, make it your own as suited to your need." Steadfastly resist every attempt of Satan to rob you of any portion of your Father's Word.

4. We profit from the Word when we make a proper discrimination between the promises of God. Many of the Lord's people are frequently guilty of spiritual theft, by which we mean that they appropriate to themselves something to which they are not entitled, but which belongs to another. "Certain covenant engagements, made with the Lord Jesus Christ, as to His elect and redeemed ones, are altogether without condition so far as we are concerned;

but many other wealthy words of the Lord contain stipulations which must be carefully regarded, or we shall not obtain the blessing. One part of my reader's diligent search must be directed toward this most important point. God will keep His promise to thee; only see thou to it that the way in which He conditions His engagement is carefully observed by thee. Only when we fulfill the requirements of a conditional promise can we expect that promise to be fulfilled to us" (C. H. Spurgeon).

Many of the Divine promises are addressed to particular characters, or, more correctly speaking, to particular graces. For example, in Psalm 25:9, the Lord declares that He will "guide in judgment" the meek; but if I am out of communion with Him, if I am following a course of self-will, if my heart is haughty, then I am not justified in taking to myself the comfort of this verse. Again, in John 15:7, the Lord tells us, "If ye abide in me, and my words abide in you, ye shall ask what ye will, and it shall be done unto you." But if I am not in experimental communion with Him, if His commands are not regulating my conduct, then my prayers will remain unanswered. While God's promises proceed from pure grace, yet it ever needs to be remembered that grace reigns "through righteousness" (Rom. 5:21) and never sets aside human responsibility. If I ignore the laws of health I must not be surprised that sickness prevents me enjoying many of God's temporal mercies: in like manner, if I neglect His precepts I have myself to blame if I fail to receive the fulfillment of many of His promises.

Let none suppose that by His promises God has obligated Himself to ignore the requirements of His holiness: He never exercises any one of His perfections at the expense of another. And let none imagine that God would be magnifying the sacrificial work of Christ were He to bestow its fruits upon impenitent and careless souls. There is a balance of truth to be preserved here; alas, that it is now so frequently lost, and that under the pretense of exalting Divine grace men are really "turning it into lasciviousness." How often one hears quoted, "Call upon me in the day of trouble: I will deliver thee" (Ps. 50:15). But that verse begins with "And," and the preceding clause is "Pay thy vows unto the most High!" Again, how frequently is "I will guide thee with mine eye" (Ps. 32:8) seized by people who pay no attention to the context! But that is God's promise to one who has confessed his "transgression" unto the Lord (verse 5). If, then, I have unconfessed sin on my conscience, and have leaned on an arm of flesh or sought help from my fellows, instead of waiting only on God (Ps. 62:5), then I have no right to count upon the Lord's guiding me with His eye—which necessarily presupposes that I am walking in close communion with Him, for I cannot see the eye of another while at a distance from him.

5. We profit from the Word when we are enabled to make God's promises our support and stay. This is one reason why God has given them to us; not only to manifest His love by making known His benevolent designs, but also to comfort our hearts and develop our faith. Had God so pleased He could have bestowed His blessings without giving us notice of His purpose. The Lord might have given us all the mercies we need without pledging Himself to do so. But in that case we could not have been believers; faith without a promise would be a foot without ground to stand upon. Our tender Father planned that we should enjoy His gifts twice over: first by faith, and then by fruition. By this means He wisely weans our hearts away from things seen and perishing and draws them onward and upward to those things which are spiritual and eternal.

If there were no promises there would not only be no faith, but no hope either. For what is hope but the expectation of the things which God has declared He will give us? Faith looks to the Word promising, hope looks to the performance thereof. Thus it was with Abraham; "Who against hope believed in hope. . .and being not weak in faith, he considered not his own body now dead, when he was about an hundred years old, neither yet the deadness of Sarah's womb; he staggered not. . .through unbelief; but was strong in faith, giving glory to God" (Rom. 4:18, 20). Thus it was with Moses: "Esteeming the reproach of Christ greater riches than the treasures in Egypt; for he had respect unto the recompense of the reward" (Heb. 11:26). Thus it was with Paul; "I believe God, that it shall be even as it was told me" (Acts 27:25). Is it so with you, dear reader? Are the promises of Him who cannot lie the resting-place of your poor heart?

6. We profit from the Word when we patiently await the fulfillment of God's promises. God promised Abraham a son, but he waited many years for the performance of it. Simeon had a promise that he should not see death till he had seen the Lord's Christ (Luke 2:26), yet it was not made good till he had one foot in the grave. There is often a long and hard winter between the sowing-time of prayer and the reaping of the answer. The Lord Jesus Him-

self has not yet received a full answer to the prayer He made in John chapter Seventeen, nineteen hundred years ago. Many of the best of God's promises to His people will not receive their richest accomplishment until they are in glory. He who has all eternity at His disposal needs not to hurry. God often makes us tarry so that patience may have "her perfect work," yet let us not distrust Him. "For the vision is yet for an appointed time, but at the end it shall speak, and not lie: though it tarry, wait for it; because it will surely come" (Hab. 2:3).

"These all died in faith, not having received the [fulfillment of the] promises but having seen them afar off, and were persuaded of them, and embraced them" (Heb. 11:13). Here is comprehended the whole work of faith: knowledge, trust, loving adherence. The "afar off" refers to the things promised; those they "saw" with the mind, discerning the substance behind the shadow, discovering in them the wisdom and goodness of God. They were "persuaded": they doubted not, but were assured of their participation in them and knew they would not disappoint them. "Embraced them" expresses their delight and veneration, the heart cleaving to them with love and cordially welcoming and entertaining them. The promises were the comfort and the stay of their souls in all their wanderings, temptations and sufferings.

Various ends are accomplished by God in delaying His execution of the promises. Not only is faith put to the proof, so that its genuineness may the more clearly appear; not only is patience developed, and hope given opportunity for exercise; but submission to the Divine will is fostered. "The weaning process is not accomplished: we are still hankering after the comforts which the Lord intends us forever to outgrow. Abraham made a great feast when his son Isaac was weaned; and, peradventure, our heavenly Father will do the same with us. Lie down, proud heart. Quit thine idols; forsake thy fond doings; and the promised peace will come unto thee" (C. H. Spurgeon).

7. We profit from the Word when we make a right use of the promises. First, in our dealings with God Himself. When we approach unto His throne, it should be to plead one of His promises. They are to form not only the foundation for our faith to rest upon, but also the substance of our requests. We must ask according to God's will if we are to be heard, and His will is revealed in those good things which He has declared He will bestow upon us. Thus

we are to lay hold of His pledged assurances, spread them before Him, and say, "Do as thou hast said" (2 Samuel 7:25). Observe how Jacob pleaded the promise in Genesis 32:12; Moses in Exodus 32:13; David in Psalm 119:58; Solomon in 1 Kings 8:25; and do thou, my Christian reader, like-wise.

Second, in the life we live in the world. In Hebrews 11:13, we not only read of the patriarchs discerning, trusting, and embracing the Divine promises, but we are also informed of the effects which they produced upon them: "and confessed that they were strangers and pilgrims in the earth," which means they made a public avowal of their faith. They acknowledged (and by their conduct demonstrated) that their interests were not in the things of this world; they had a satisfying portion in the promises they had appropriated. Their hearts were set upon things above; for where a man's heart is, there will his treasure be also.

"Having therefore these promises, dearly beloved, let us cleanse ourselves from all filthiness of the flesh and spirit, perfecting holiness in the fear of God" (2 Cor. 7:1); that is the effect they should produce in us, and will if faith really lays hold of them. "Whereby are given unto us exceeding great and precious promises: that by these ye might be partakers of the divine nature, having escaped the corruption that is in the world through lust" (2 Pet. 1:4). Now the Gospel and the precious promises, being graciously bestowed and powerfully applied, have an influence on purity of heart and behavior, and teach men to deny ungodliness and worldly lusts, and to live soberly, righteously, and godly. Such are the powerful effects of gospel promises under the Divine influence as to make men inwardly partakers of the Divine nature and outwardly to abstain from and avoid the prevailing corruptions and vices of the times.

Chapter 9
The Scriptures and Joy

The ungodly are ever seeking after joy, but they do not find it: they busy and weary themselves in the pursuit of it, yet all in vain. Their hearts being turned from the Lord, they look downward for joy, where it is not; rejecting the substance, they diligently run after the shadow, only to be mocked by it. It is the sovereign decree of heaven that nothing can make sinners truly happy but God in Christ; but this they will not believe, and therefore they go from creature to creature, from one broken cistern to another, inquiring where the best joy is to be found. Each worldly thing which attracts them says, It is found in me; but soon it disappoints. Nevertheless, they go on seeking it afresh today in the very thing which deceived them yesterday. If after many trials they discover the emptiness of one creature comfort, then they turn to another, only to verify our Lord's word, "Whosoever drinketh of this water shall thirst again" (John 4:13).

Going now to the other extreme: there are some Christians who suppose it to be sinful to rejoice. No doubt many of our readers will be surprised to hear this but let them be thankful they have been brought up in sunnier surroundings, and bear with us while we labor with those less favored. Some have been taught—largely by implication and example, rather than by plain inculcation—that it is their duty to be gloomy. They imagine that feelings of joy are produced by the Devil appearing as an angel of light. They conclude that it is well-nigh a species of wickedness to be happy in such a world of sin as we are in. They think it presumptuous to rejoice in the knowledge of sins forgiven, and if they see young Christians so doing they tell them it will not be long before they are floundering in the Slough of Despond. To all such we tenderly urge the prayerful pondering of the remainder of this chapter.

"Rejoice evermore" (1 Thess. 5:16). It surely cannot be unsafe to do what God has commanded us. The Lord has placed no embargo on rejoicing. No, it is Satan who strives to make us hang up our harps. There is no precept in Scripture bidding us "Grieve in the Lord always: and again I say, Grieve"; but there is an exhortation which bids us, "Rejoice in the Lord, O ye righteous: for praise is comely for the upright" (Ps. 33:1). Reader, if you are a real Christian (and it is high time you tested yourself by Scripture and made sure of this point), then Christ is yours, all that is in Him is yours. He bids you "Eat, O friends; drink, yea, drink abundantly, O beloved" (Song of Sol. 5:1): the only sin you may commit against His banquet of love is to stint yourself. "Let your soul delight itself in fatness"(Isa. 55:2) is spoken not to those already in heaven but to saints still on earth. This leads us to say that:

1. We profit from the Word when we perceive that joy is a duty. "Rejoice in the Lord always: and again I say, Rejoice" (Phil. 4:4). The Holy Spirit here speaks of rejoicing as a personal, present and permanent duty for the people of God to carry out. The Lord has not left it to our option whether we should be glad or sad, but has made happiness an obligation. Not to rejoice is a sin of omission. Next time you meet with a radiant Christian, do not chide him, ye dwellers in Doubting Castle, but chide yourselves; instead of being ready to call into question the Divine spring of his mirth, judge yourself for your doleful state.

It is not a carnal joy which we are here urging, by which we mean a joy which comes from carnal sources. It is useless to seek joy in earthly riches, for frequently they take to themselves wings and fly away. Some seek their joy in the family circle, but that remains entire for only a few years at most. No, if we are to "rejoice evermore" it must be in an object that lasts for evermore. Nor is it a fanatical joy we have reference to. There are some with an excitable nature who are happy only when they are half out of their minds; but terrible is the reaction. No, it is an intelligent, steady, heart delight in God Himself. Every attribute of God, when contemplated by faith, will make the heart sing. Every doctrine of the Gospel, when truly apprehended, will call forth gladness and praise.

Joy is a matter of Christian duty. Perhaps the reader is ready to exclaim, My emotions of joy and sorrow are not under my control; I cannot help being glad or sad as circumstances dictate. But we repeat, "Rejoice in the Lord" is a Divine command, and to a large extent obedience to it lies in one's own power. I am responsible to control my emotions. True I cannot help being sorrowful in the presence of sorrowful thoughts, but I can refuse to let my mind dwell upon them. I can pour out my heart for relief unto the Lord, and cast my burden upon Him. I can seek grace to meditate upon His goodness, His promises, the glorious future awaiting me. I have to decide whether I will go and stand in the light or hide among the shadows. Not to rejoice in the Lord is more than a misfortune, it is a fault which needs to be confessed and forsaken.

2. We profit from the Word when we learn the secret of true joy. That secret is revealed in I John 1:3,4: Truly our fellowship is with the Father, and with his Son Jesus Christ. And these things write we unto you, that your joy may be full." When we consider the littleness of our fellowship with God, the shallowness of it, it is not to be wondered at that so many Christians are comparatively joyless. We sometimes sing, "Oh happy day that fixed my choice on Thee, my Savior and my God! Well may this glowing heart rejoice and tell its raptures all abroad." Yes, but if that happiness is to be maintained there must be a continued steadfast occupation of the heart and mind with Christ. It is only where there is much faith and consequent love that there is much joy.

"Rejoice in the Lord always." There is no other object in which we can rejoice "always." Everything else varies and is inconstant. What pleases us today may pall on us tomorrow. But the Lord is always the same, to be enjoyed in seasons of adversity as much as in seasons of prosperity. As an aid to this, the very next verse says, "Let your moderation be known unto all men. The Lord is at hand" (Phil. 4:5). Be temperate in connection with all external things; do not be taken with them when they seem most pleasing, nor troubled when displeasing. Be not exalted when the world smiles upon you, nor dejected when it scowls. Maintain a stoical indifference to outward comforts: why be so occupied with them when the Lord Himself "is at hand"? If persecution be violent, if temporal losses be heavy, the Lord is "a very present help in trouble" (Ps. 46:1)—ready to support and succor those who cast themselves upon Him. He will care for you, so "be anxious for nothing" (Phil. 4:6). Worldlings are haunted with carking cares, but the Christian should not be.

"These things have I spoken unto you, that my joy might remain in you, and that your joy might be full" (John 15:11). As these precious words of Christ are pondered by the mind and treasured in the heart, they cannot but produce joy. A rejoicing heart comes from an increasing knowledge of and love for the truth as it is in Jesus. "Thy words were found, and I did eat them; and thy word was unto me the joy and rejoicing of mine heart" (Jer. 15:16). Yes, it is by feeding and feasting upon the words of the Lord that the soul is made fat, and we are made to sing and make melody in our hearts unto Him.

"Then will I go unto the altar of God, unto God my exceeding joy" (Ps. 43:4). As Spurgeon well said, "With what exultation should believers draw near unto Christ, who is the antitype of the altar! Clearer light should give greater intensity of desire. It was not the altar as such that the Psalmist cared for, for he was no believer in the heathenism of ritualism: his soul desired spiritual fellowship, fellowship with God Himself in very deed. What are all the rites of worship unless the Lord be in them; what, indeed, but empty shells and dry husks? Note the holy rapture with which David regards his Lord! He is not his joy alone, but his exceeding joy; not the fountain of joy, the giver of joy, or the maintainer of joy, but that joy itself. The margin hath it, "The gladness of my joy"; i.e. the soul, the essence, the very bowels of my joy."

"Although the fig tree shall not blossom, neither shall fruit be in the vines; the labor of the olive shall fail, and the fields shall yield no meat; the flock shall be cut off from the fold, and there shall be no herd in the stalls: yet I will rejoice in the Lord, I will joy in the God of my salvation" (Hab. 3:17,18). That is something of which the worldling knows nothing; alas, that it is an experience to which so many professing Christians are strangers! It is in God that the fount of spiritual and everlasting joy originates; from Him it all flows forth. This was acknowledged of old by the Church when she said, "All my springs are in thee" (Ps. 87:7). Happy the soul who has been truly taught this secret!

3. We profit from the Word when we are taught the great value of joy. Joy is to the soul what wings are to the bird, enabling us to soar above the things of earth. This is brought out plainly in Nehemiah 8:10: "The joy of the Lord is your strength." The days of Nehemiah marked a turning-point in the history of Israel. A remnant had been freed from Babylon and returned to Palestine. The Law, long ignored by the captives, was now to be established again as the rule of the newly-formed commonwealth. There had come a remembrance of the many sins of the past, and tears not unnaturally mingled with the thankfulness that they were again a

nation, having a Divine worship and a Divine Law in their midst. Their leader, knowing full well that if the spirit of the people began to flag they could not face and conquer the difficulties of their position, said to them: "This day is holy unto the Lord: (this feast we are keeping is a day of devout worship; therefore, mourn not), neither be ye sorry, for the joy of the Lord is your strength."

Confession of sin and mourning over the same have their place, and communion with God cannot be maintained without them. Nevertheless, when true repentance has been exercised, and things put right with God, we must forget "those things which are behind" and reach forth unto "those things which are before" (Phil. 3:13). And we can only press forward with alacrity as our hearts are joyful. How heavy the steps of him who approaches the place where a loved one lies cold in death! How energetic his movements as he goes forth to meet his bride! Lamentation unfits for the battles of life. Where there is despair there is no longer power for obedience. If there be no joy, there can be no worship.

My dear readers, there are tasks needing to be performed, service to others requiring to be rendered, temptations to be overcome, battles to be fought; and we are only experimentally fitted for them as our hearts are rejoicing in the Lord. If our souls are resting in Christ, if our hearts are filled with a tranquil gladness, work will be easy, duties pleasant, sorrow bearable, endurance possible. Neither contrite remembrance of past failures nor vehement resolutions will carry us through. If the arm is to smite with vigor, it must smite at the bidding of a light heart. Of the Savior Himself it is recorded, "Who for the joy that was set before him endured the cross, despising the shame" (Heb. 12:2).

4. We profit from the Word when we attend to the root of joy. The spring of joy is faith: "Now the God of hope fill you with all peace and joy in believing" (Rom. 15:13). There is a wondrous provision in the Gospel, both by what it takes from us and what it brings to us, to give a calm and settled glow to the Christian's heart. It takes away the load of guilt by speaking peace to the stricken conscience. It removes the dread of God and the terror of death which weighs on the soul while it is under condemnation. It gives us God Himself as the portion of our hearts, as the object of our communion. The Gospel works joy, because the soul is at rest in God. But these blessings become our own only by personal appropriation. Faith must receive them, and when it does so the heart is

filled with peace and joy. And the secret of sustained joy is to keep the channel open, to continue as we began. It is unbelief which clogs the channel. If there be but little heat around the bulb of the thermometer, no wonder that the mercury marks so low a degree. If there is a weak faith, joy cannot be strong. Daily do we need to pray for a fresh realization of the preciousness of the Gospel, a fresh appropriation of its blessed contents; and then there will be a renewing of our joy.

5. We profit from the Word when we are careful to maintain our joy. "Joy in the Holy Spirit" is altogether different from a natural buoyancy of Spirit. It is the product of the Comforter dwelling in our hearts and bodies, revealing Christ to us, answering all our need for pardon and cleansing, and so Setting us at peace with God; and forming Christ in us, so that He reigns in our souls, subduing us to His control. There are no circumstances of trial and temptation in which we may refrain from it, for the command is, "Rejoice in the Lord always." He who gave this command knows all about the dark side of our lives, the sins and sorrows which beset us, the "much tribulation" through which we must enter the kingdom of God. Natural hilarity leaves the woes of our earthly lot out of its reckoning. It soon relaxes in the presence of life's hardships: it cannot survive the loss of friends or health. But the joy to which we are exhorted is not limited to any set of circumstances or type of temperament; nor does it fluctuate with our varying moods and fortunes.

Nature may assert itself in the subjects of it, as even Jesus wept at the grave of Lazarus. Nevertheless, they can exclaim with Paul, "As sorrowful, yet always rejoicing" (2 Cor. 6:10). The Christian may be loaded with heavy responsibilities, his life may have a series of reverses, his plans may be thwarted and his hopes blighted, the grave may close over the loved ones who gave his earthly life its cheer and sweetness, and yet, under all his disappointments and sorrows, his Lord still bids him "Rejoice." Behold the apostles in Philippi's prison, in the innermost dungeon, with feet fast in the stocks, and backs bleeding and smarting from the terrible scourging they had received. How were they occupied? In grumbling and growling? in asking what they had done to deserve such treatment? No! At midnight Paul and Silas prayed and sang praises unto God" (Acts 16:25). There was no sin in their lives, they were walking obediently, and so the Holy Spirit was free to take of the things of Christ, and show them unto their hearts, so that they were filled to overflowing. If we are to maintain our joy, we must keep from grieving the Holy Spirit.

When Christ is supreme in the heart, joy fills it. When He is Lord of every desire, the Source of every motive, the Subjugator of every lust, then will joy fill the heart and praise ascend from the lips. The possession of this involves taking up the cross every hour of the day; God has so ordered it that we cannot have the one without the other. Self-sacrifice, the cutting off of a right hand, the plucking out of a right eye, are the avenues through which the Spirit enters the soul, bringing with Him the joys of God's approving smile and the assurance of His love and abiding presence. Much also depends upon the spirit in which we enter the world each day. If we expect people to pet and pamper us, disappointment will make us fretful. If we desire our pride to be ministered to, we are dejected when it is not. The secret of happiness is forgetting self and seeking to minister to the happiness of others. "It is more blessed to give than to receive," so it is a happier thing to minister to others than to be ministered to.

6. We profit from the Word when we are sedulous in avoiding the hindrances to joy. Why is it that so many Christians have so little joy? Are they not all born children of the light and of the day? This term "light," which is so often used in Scripture to describe to us the nature of God, our relations to Him and our future destiny, is most suggestive of joy and gladness. What other thing in nature is as beneficent and beautiful as the light? "God is light, and in Him is no darkness at all (1 John 1:5). It is only as we walk with God, in the light, that the heart can truly be joyous. It is the deliberate allowing of things which mar our fellowship with Him that chills and darkens our souls. It is the indulgence of the flesh, the fraternizing with the world, the entering of forbidden paths which blight our spiritual lives and make us cheerless.

David had to cry, "Restore unto me the joy of thy salvation" (Ps. 51:12). He had grown lax and self-indulgent. Temptation presented itself and he had no power to resist. He yielded, and one sin led to another. He was a backslider, out of touch with God. Unconfessed sin lay heavy on his conscience. Oh my brethren and sisters, if we are to be kept from such a fall, if we are not to lose our joy, then self must be denied, the affections and lusts of the flesh crucified. We must ever be on our watch against temptation. We must spend much time upon our knees. We must drink frequently from the Fountain of living waters. We must be out-and-out for the Lord.

7. We profit from the Word when we diligently preserve the balance between sorrow and joy. If the Christian faith has a marked adaptation to produce joy, it has an almost equal design and tendency to produce sorrow—a sorrow that is solemn, manly, noble. "As sorrowful, yet always rejoicing" (2 Cor. 6:10) is the rule of the Christian's life. If faith casts its light upon our condition, our nature, our sins, sadness must be one of the effects. There is nothing more contemptible in itself, and there is no surer mark of a superficial character and trivial round of occupation, than unshaded gladness, that rests on no deep foundations of quiet, patient grief—grief because I know what I am and what I ought to be; grief because I look out on the world and see hell's fire burning at the back of mirth and laughter, and know what it is that men are hurrying to.

He who is anointed with the oil of gladness above His fellows (Ps. 45:7) was also "the man of sorrows and acquainted with grief." And both of these characters are (in measure) repeated in the operations of His Gospel upon every heart that really receives it. And if, on the one hand, by the fears it removes from us and the hopes it breathes into us, and the fellowship into which it introduces us, we are anointed with the oil of gladness; on the other hand, by the sense of our own vileness which it teaches us, by the conflict between the flesh and the Spirit, there is infused a sadness which finds expression in "O wretched man that I am!" (Rom. 7:24). These two are not contradictory but complementary. The Lamb must be eaten with "bitter herbs" (Ex. 12:8).

Chapter 10
The Scriptures and Love

In earlier chapters we have sought to point out some of the ways by which we may ascertain whether or not our reading and searching of the Scriptures are really being blessed to our souls. Many are deceived on this matter, mistaking an eagerness to acquire knowledge for a spiritual love of the Truth (2 Thess. 2:10), and assuming that addition to their store of learning is the same thing as growth in grace. A great deal depends upon the end or aim we have before us when turning to God's Word. If it be simply to familiarize ourselves with its contents and become better versed in its details, it is likely that the garden of our souls will remain barren; but if with the prayerful desire to be rebuked and corrected by the Word, to be searched by the Spirit, to conform our hearts to its holy requirements, then we may expect a Divine blessing.

In the preceding chapters we have endeavored to single out the vital things by which we may discover what progress we are making in personal godliness. Various criteria have been given, which it becomes both writer and reader honestly to measure themselves by. We have pressed such tests as: Am I acquiring a greater hatred of sin, and a practical deliverance from its power and pollution? Am I obtaining a deeper acquaintance with God and His Christ? Is my prayer-life healthier? Are my good works more abundant? Is my obedience fuller and gladder? Am I more separated from the world in my affections and ways? Am I learning to make a right and profitable use of God's promises, and so delighting myself in Him that His joy is my daily strength? Unless I can truthfully say that these are (in some measure) my experience, then it is greatly to be feared that my study of the Scriptures is profiting me little or nothing.

It hardly seems fitting that these chapters should be concluded until one has been devoted to the consideration of Christian love. The extent to which this spiritual grace is, or is not, being cultivated and regulated affords another index to the measure in which my perusal of God's Word is helping me spiritually. No one can read the Scriptures with any measure of attention without discovering how much they have to say about love, and therefore it behooves each one of us prayerfully and carefully to ascertain whether or not his or her love be really a spiritual one, and whether it be in a healthy state and is being exercised aright.

The subject of Christian love is far too comprehensive to consider all its varied phases within the compass of a single chapter. Properly we should begin with contemplating the exercise of our love toward God and His Christ, but as this has been at least touched upon in preceding chapters we shall now waive it. Much too, might be said about the natural love which we owe to our fellow-men, who belong to the same family as we do, but there is less need to write on that theme than on what is now before our mind. Here we propose to confine our attention to spiritual love to the brethren, the brethren of Christ.

1. We profit from the Word when we perceive the great importance of Christian love. Nowhere is this brought out more emphatically than in 1 Corinthians chapter 13. There the Holy Spirit tells us that though a professing Christian can speak fluently and eloquently upon Divine things, if has not love, he is like metal, which, though it makes a noise when struck, is lifeless. That though he can prophesy, understand all mysteries and knowledge, and has faith which brings miracles to pass, yet if he be lacking in love, he is spiritually a nonentity. Yea, that though he be so benevolent as to give all his worldly possessions to feed the poor, and yield his body to a martyr's death, yet if he have not love, it profits him nothing. How high a value is here placed upon love, and how essential for me to make sure I possess it!

Said our Lord, "By this shall all men know that ye are my disciples, if ye have love one to another" (John 13:35). By Christ's making it the badge of Christian discipleship, we see again the great importance of love. It is an essential test of the genuineness of our profession: we cannot love Christ unless we love His brethren, for they are all bound up in the same "bundle of life" (1 Samuel 25:29) with Him. Love to those whom He has redeemed is a sure evidence of spiritual and supernatural love to the Lord Jesus Himself. Where the Holy Spirit has wrought a supernatural birth, He will draw forth that nature into exercise, He will produce in the hearts and lives and conduct of the saints supernatural graces, one of which is loving all who are Christ's for Christ's sake.

2. We profit from the Word when we learn to detect the sad perversions of Christian love. As water will not rise above its own level, so the natural man is incapable of understanding, still less appreciating, that which is spiritual (1 Cor. 2:14). Therefore we should not be surprised when unregenerate professors mistake human sentimentality and carnal pleasantries for spiritual love. But sad it is to see some of God's own people living on so low a plane that they confuse human amiability and affability with the queen of the Christian graces. While it is true that spiritual love is characterized by meekness and gentleness, yet is it something very different from and vastly superior to the courtesies and kindnesses of the flesh.

How many a doting father has withheld the rod from his children, under the mistaken notion that real affection for them and the chastising of them were incompatible! How many a foolish mother, who disdained all corporal punishment, has boasted that "love" rules in her home! One of the most trying experiences of the writer, in his extensive travels, has been to spend a season in homes where the children have been completely spoilt. It is a wicked perversion of the word "love" to apply it to moral laxity and parental looseness. But this same pernicious idea rules the minds of many people in other connections and relations. If a servant of God rebukes their fleshly and worldly ways, if he presses the uncompromising claims of God, he is at once charged with being "lacking in love." Oh, how terribly are multitudes deceived by Satan on this important subject!

3. We profit from the Word when we are taught the true nature of Christian love. Christian love is a spiritual grace abiding in the souls of the saints alongside faith and hope (1 Cor. 13:13). It is a holy disposition wrought in them when they are regenerated (1 John 5:1). It is nothing less than the love of God shed abroad in their hearts by the Holy Spirit (Rom. 5:5). It is a righteous principle which seeks the highest good of others. It is the very reverse of that principle of self-love and self-seeking which is in us by nature. It is not only an affectionate regard of all who bear the image of Christ, but also a powerful desire to promote their welfare. It is not a fickle sentiment which is easily offended, but an abiding dynamic which "many waters" of cold indifference or "floods"

of disapproval can neither quench nor drown (Song of Sol. 8:7). Though coming far short in degree it is the same in essence as His of whom we read, "Having loved his own which were in the world, he loved them unto the end" (John 13:1).

There is no safer and surer way of obtaining a right conception of the nature of Christian love than by making a thorough study of its perfect exemplification in and by the Lord Jesus. When we say a "thorough study," we mean the taking of a comprehensive survey of all that is recorded of Him in the four Gospels, and not the limiting of ourselves to a few favorite passages or incidents. As this is done, we discover that His love was not only benevolent and magnanimous, thoughtful and gentle, unselfish and self-sacrificing, patient and unchanging, but that many other elements also entered into it. Love could deny an urgent request (John 11:6), rebuke His mother (John 2:4), use a whip (John 2:15), severely upbraid His doubting disciples (Luke 24:25), and denounce hypocrites (Matt. 23:13-33). Love can be stern (Matt. 16:23), yea, angry (Mark 3:5). Spiritual love is a holy thing: it is faithful to God; it is uncompromising toward all that is evil.

4. We profit from the Word when we discover that Christian love is a Divine communication. "We know that we have passed from death unto life, because we love the brethren" (1 John 3:14). "Love to the brethren is the fruit and effect of a new and supernatural birth, wrought in our souls by the Holy Spirit, as the blessed evidence of our having been chosen in Christ by the Divine Father, before the world was. To love Christ and His, and our brethren in Him, is congenial to that Divine nature He hath made us the partakers of by His Holy Spirit. .... This love of the brethren must be a peculiar love, such as none but the regenerate are the subjects of, and which none but they can exercise, or the apostle would not have so particularly mentioned it; it is such that those who have it not are in a state of unregeneracy; so it follows, "he that loveth not his brother abideth in death" " (S. E. Pierce).

Love for the brethren is far, far more than finding agreeable the society of those whose temperaments are similar to or whose views accord with my own. It pertains not to mere nature, but is a spiritual and supernatural thing. It is the heart being drawn out to those in whom I perceive something of Christ. Thus it is very much more than a party spirit; it embraces all in whom I can see the image of God's Son. It is, therefore, a loving them for Christ's sake, for what I see of Christ in them. It is the Holy Spirit within attracting and alluring me with Christ indwelling my brethren and sisters. Thus real Christian love is not only a Divine gift, but is altogether dependent upon God for its invigoration and exercise. We need to pray daily that the Holy Spirit will call forth into action and manifestation, toward both God and His people, that love which He has shed abroad in our hearts.

5. We profit from the Word when we rightly exercise Christian love. This is done, not by seeking to please our brethren and ingratiate ourselves in their esteem, but when we truly seek their highest good. "By this we know that we love the children of God, when we love God, and keep his commandments" (1 John 5:2). What is the real test of my personal love to God Himself? It is my keeping of His commandments (see John 14:15, 21, 24; 15:10,14). The genuineness and strength of my love to God are not to be measured by my words, nor by the lustiness with which I sing His praises, but by my obedience to His Word. The same principle holds good in my relations with my brethren.

"By this we know that we love the children of God, when we love God, and keep His commandments." If I am glossing over the faults of my brethren and sisters, if I am walking with them in a course of self-will and self-pleasing, then I am not "loving" them. "Thou shalt not hate thy brother in thine heart: thou shalt in any wise rebuke thy neighbor, and not suffer sin upon him" (Lev. 19:17). Love is to be exercised in a Divine way, and never at the expense of my failing to love God; in fact, it is only when God has His proper place in my heart that spiritual love can be exercised by me toward my brethren. True spiritual love does not consist in gratifying them, but in pleasing God and helping them; and I can only help them in the path of God's commandments.

Petting and pampering one another is not brotherly love; exhorting one another to press forward in the race that is set before us, and speaking words (enforced by the example of our daily walk) which will encourage them to "look off unto Jesus," would be much more helpful. Brotherly love is a holy thing, and not a fleshly sentiment or a loose indifference as to the path we are treading. God's "commandments" are expressions of His love, as well as of His authority, and to ignore them, even while seeking to be kindly affectionate one to another, is not "love" at all. The exercise of love is to be in strict conformity to the revealed will of God. We are to love "in the truth" (3 John 1).

6. We profit from the Word when we are taught the varied manifestations of Christian love. To love our brethren and manifest the love in all kinds of ways is our bounden duty. But at no point can we do this more truly and effectually, and with less affection and ostentation, than by having fellowship with them at the throne of grace. There are brethren and sisters in Christ in the four corners of the earth, about the details of whose trials and conflicts, temptations and sorrows, I know nothing; yet I can express my love for them, and pour out my heart before God on their behalf, by earnest supplication and intercession. In no other way can the Christian more manifest his affectionate regard toward his fellow-pilgrims than by using all his interests in the Lord Jesus in their behalf, in-treating His mercies and favors unto them.

"Whoso hath this world's good, and seeth his brother have need, and shutteth up his bowels of compassion from him, how dwelleth the love of God in him? My little children, let us not love in word, neither in tongue; but in deed and in truth" (1 John 3:17,18). Many of God's people are very poor in this world's goods. Sometimes they wonder why it is so; it is a great trial to them. One reason why the Lord permits this is that others of His Saints may have their compassion drawn out and minister to their temporal needs from the abundance with which God has furnished them. Real love is intensely practical: it considers no office too mean, no task too humbling, where the sufferings of a brother can be relieved. When the Lord of love was here upon earth, He had thought for the bodily hunger of the multitude and the comfort of His disciples" feet!

But there are some of the Lord's people so poor that they have very little indeed to share with others. What, then, may they do? Why, make the spiritual concerns of all the saints their own; interest themselves on their behalf at the throne of grace! We know by our own cases and circumstances what the feelings, sorrows, and complaints of other saints must be the subjects of. We know from sad experience how easy it is to give way to a spirit of discontent and murmuring. But we also know how, when we have cried unto the Lord for His quieting hand to be laid upon us, and when He has brought some precious promise to our remembrance, what peace and comfort have come to our heart. Then let us beg Him to be equally gracious to all His distressed saints. Let us seek to make their burdens our own, and weep with them that weep, as well as rejoice with them that rejoice. Thus shall we express real love for their persons in Christ by entreating their Lord and our Lord to remember them with everlasting kindness.

This is how the Lord Jesus is now manifesting His love to His saints: "He ever liveth to make intercession for them" (Heb. 7:25). He makes their cause and care His own. He is entreating the Father on their behalf. None is forgotten by Him: every lone sheep is borne upon the heart of the Good Shepherd. Thus, by expressing our love to the brethren in daily prayers for the supply of their varied needs, we are brought into fellowship with our great High Priest. Not only so, but the saints will be endeared to us thereby: our very praying for them as the beloved of God will increase our love and esteem for them as such. We cannot carry them on our hearts before the throne of grace without cherishing in our own hearts a real affection for them. The best way of overcoming a bitter spirit to a brother who has offended is to be much in prayer for him.

7. We profit from the Word when we are taught the proper cultivation of Christian love. We suggest two or three rules for this. First, recognizing at the outset that just as there is much in you (in me) which will severely try the love of the brethren, so there will be not a little in them to test our love. "Forbearing one another in love" (Eph. 4:3) is a great admonition on this subject which each of us needs to lay to heart. It is surely striking to note that the very first quality of spiritual love named in , Corinthians 13 is that it "suffereth long" (verse 4).

Second, the best way to cultivate any virtue or grace is to exercise it. Talking and theorizing about it avails nothing unless it be carried into action. Many are the complaints heard today about the littleness of the love which is being manifested in many places: that is all the more reason why I should seek to see? a better example! Suffer not the coldness and unkindliness of others to dampen your love, but "overcome evil with good" (Romans. 12:21). Prayerfully ponder 1 Corinthians 13 at least once a week.

Third, above all, see to it that your own heart basks in the light and warmth of God's love. Like begets like. The more you are truly occupied with the unwearying, unfailing, unfathomable love of Christ to you, the more will your heart be drawn out in love to those who are His. A beautiful illustration of this is found in the fact that the particular apostle who wrote most upon brotherly love was he who leaned upon the Master's bosom. The Lord grant all requisite grace to both reader and writer (than whom none more needs to heed them) to observe these rules, to the praise of the glory of His grace, and to the good of His beloved people.

Divine Healing: Is It Scriptural?

Arthur W. Pink

Contents

Introduction	169
Chapter 1 The Positive Side	174
Chapter 2 The Subject of Health	175
Chapter 3 The Duties and Privileges of Christian Illness	179
Chapter 4 2 Chronicles 7:14 Considered	181
Chapter 5 The Pertinence of Matthew 9:29	185
Chapter 6 Appendix on James 5:14-16	189

Introduction

Every once in a while we receive an inquiry or a request for help on this subject, usually from one who has come into contact with some belonging to a cult which gives prominence to "Divine healing," to the removal of physical ills without the aid of a doctor and medicine, in response to faith and prayer. Such inquiring friends are generally more or less perplexed. They have heard nothing on the subject in their own churches and feel they are more or less in the dark on the matter. Those who press this "Divine healing" teaching upon them appear to be ill-balanced people and not at all orthodox in doctrine. If they are induced to attend their meetings they are not favorably impressed, and sense that something is wrong. The absence of reverence, the allowing of women to take part in the services before a mixed congregation, the prominence of the spectacular element, and the general spirit of excitement which prevails, makes the normal child of God feel quite out of place in such a gathering. The zeal displayed does not appear to be according to knowledge and the fervid emotionalism strikes him as being "strange fire" (Lev. 10:1)—not kindled at the Divine altar.

But what of their teaching on "Divine healing?" Is it scriptural or unscriptural? This is a question which it is not easy to answer in a single sentence. Many passages on healing may be cited from God's Word, but that raises the question of their interpretation—in accord with the context and also in harmony with the general Analogy of Faith: as it also calls for a careful examination of all inferences drawn from and conclusions based upon those passages. Moreover, these modern cults who stress "Divine healing" are by no means uniform in their teaching thereon, some being more radical and extreme than others, so that the refutation of one erroneous presentation of this subject would not hold good of a similar error in an entirely different dress. Though familiar with all the principal varieties of them, we do not propose to waste the reader's time by taking them up seriatim but rather deal with the broad principles which apply to them all.

First it must be said that much of the teaching which has been given out on this subject is decidedly unscriptural. For example, the majority of those who emphasize "Divine healing" insist that it was "in the Atonement," that on the Cross Christ was as truly our sickness-bearer as our sin-bearer, that He purchased healing for the body as well as salvation for the soul, and that therefore every Christian has the same right to appropriate by faith the cure of bodily disorders as he has forgiveness for his transgressions. In support of this contention appeal is made to Christ who "healed all that were sick, that it might be fulfilled which was spoken by Isaiah the prophet: Himself took our infirmities and bare our sicknesses" (Matt. 8:16, 17). Here is where the expositor is needed if the unlettered and unstable are to be preserved from jumping to an erroneous conclusion, where the mere sound of the words is likely to convey a wrong impression unless their sense be carefully ascertained—just as, "the dead know not anything" (Eccl. 9:5) is not to be understood absolutely, as though they who have departed this life are in a state of utter unconsciousness.

Had those words "Christ bare our sicknesses" occurred in some passage in the Acts or Epistles where one of the apostles was explaining the purpose and character of Christ's death, then we should have been obliged to regard them as meaning that the Lord Jesus vicariously endured the sicknesses of His people while on the Cross, though this would present a very great difficulty, for there is no hint anywhere in the Word that the Redeemer experienced any illness at that time. But instead, Matthew 8:16, 17 has reference to what transpired during the days of His public ministry, the meaning of which we take to be as follows. Christ employed not the virtue that was in Him to cure infirmity and sickness as a matter of mere power, but in deep pity and tenderness He entered into the condition of the sufferer. The great Physician was no unfeeling stoic, but took upon His own spirit the sorrows and pains of those to whom He ministered. His miracles of healing cost Him much in the way of sympathy and endurance. Thus He "sighed" (Mark 7:34) when He loosed the tongue of the dumb, "wept" by the grave of Lazarus, and was conscious of virtue going out of Him (Mark 5:30) as He cured another. By a compassion, such as we are strangers to, He was afflicted by their afflictions.

That the interpretation we have given above (briefly suggested by the Puritan, Thomas Goodwin) is the correct meaning of "Himself took our infirmities and bare our sicknesses" appears from several considerations. If those words signified what the "Divine healing" cults say they do, then they mean that in His act of healing the sick Christ was then making atonement, which is absurd on the face of it. Again, if the healing of the body were a redemptive right which faith may humbly but boldly claim, then it necessarily follows that the believer should never die, for every time he fell ill he could plead before God the sacrifice of His Son and claim healing. In such a case, why did not Paul exhort Timothy to exercise faith in the Atonement rather than bid him "use a little wine for his stomach's sake" (1 Tim. 5:23), and why did he leave Trophimus at "Miletum sick" (2 Tim. 4:20)? A glorified body, as well as soul, is the fruit of Christ's atonement, but for that the believer has to wait God's appointed time.

One error leads to another: most of those who teach that Divine healing is in the Atonement argue that therefore it must constitute an essential element in and part of the Gospel, and thus their favorite slogan is: "Christ our Savior, Christ our Sanctifier, Christ our Healer, Christ our Coming King," and hence "the Fourfold Gospel" is the leading caption of most of them. But such a contention will not bear the light of Holy Writ. In the book of Acts we find the apostles preaching the Gospel of God both to Jews and Gentiles, yet, though in the course of their ministry miracles of healing were performed by them (to authenticate their mission, for none of the N. T. had then been written), yet nowhere did the removal of physical maladies form part of their message. In 1 Corinthians 15:1-3 a brief summary of the Gospel is given, namely, that "Christ died for our sins according to the Scriptures, and that He was buried, and that He rose again the third day"—mark the omission of His dying for our sicknesses! In Romans we are furnished with a systematic and full unfolding of "the Gospel of God" (see 1:1), yet "healing" of bodily ills is never referred to.

If it were true that Christ made atonement for our sicknesses as well as our sins, then it would follow that all bodily disorders are the immediate consequence of some iniquity. We say, "immediate consequence," for of course it is readily granted that all the ills which man is heir to are so many effects and results of the great transgression of our first parents. It is only reasonable to conclude that had sin never entered this world suffering in any form had been unknown here, for we know that in Heaven the absence of the former ensures the absence of the latter. Thus there is a vital difference between saying that a physical disorder which occasions great discomfort and pain finds its remote cause in the tragedy of Eden, and affirming that it is the direct result of the person's own wrong doing, as most of the "Divine healing" cults insist. Our Lord's reply to His disciples in John 9:2, 3 expressly forbids any such sweeping conclusion. There is much suffering, especially among children, which is due to ignorant and innocent breaking of natural laws rather than to violation of the Moral Law. Moreover, if this contention of "Divine healing" were valid, we should be obliged to conclude that every sickness severed the soul from communion with God, which is falsified by the experiences of many of the saintliest persons who ever trod this earth.

Those who hold that Christ made atonement for our sicknesses as well as for our sins are quite consistent in maintaining that deliverance from the former must be obtained in precisely the same way as salvation from the latter: that the sole means must be the exercise of faith, without the introduction or addition of any works or doings of our own. Thus the "Divine healing" cults teach that the service of a physician or the aid of drugs is as much a setting aside of the finished work of Christ as reliance upon baptism or deeds of charity for the securing of pardon would be. The untenability of this logical inference will at once show that while in some cases God was pleased to cure the sick without means, yet in other instances He both appointed and blessed the use of means. For the healing of the bitter waters of Marah, Moses was instructed to cast into them a tree which "the Lord showed him" (Ex. 15:25). When God promised to heal Hezekiah who was sick unto death, Isaiah bade the king "take a lump of figs" and we are told "they took and laid it on the boil, and he recovered" (2 Kings 20:7). So with Timothy in 1 Timothy 5:23.

We are certainly not prepared to hold any brief in defense of the present-day medical fraternity as a whole. The greed for gold, the love of novelty (experimentation), the deterioration of moral character in all walks of life, fails to inspire confidence in any class or clique, and the writer for one would prefer to suffer pain than place himself at the mercy of the average surgeon. Yet this does not mean that we regard all medical practitioners as either charlatans or knaves, still less do we believe with "Faith-healing" fanatics that they are the special emissaries of Satan. The Holy Spirit would never have termed Luke "the beloved physician" (Col. 4:14) had he been employed in the service of the Devil.

Arthur W. Pink

Chapter 1
The Positive Side

Having exposed the cardinal errors promulgated by the "Divine healing" cults, we turn now to the positive side of the subject. And there is pressing need to do so, for the pulpit has failed grievously here as in so many other directions. Of old God complained, "My people are destroyed for lack of knowledge" (Hos. 4:6), and history has repeated itself. It was prophesied, "Behold, the days come, saith the Lord God, that I will send a famine in the land, not a famine of bread nor a thirst for water, but of hearing the words of the Lord" (Amos 8:11), and that fearful prediction is now in course of fulfillment. In the vast majority of places rank error rather than the Truth is being given out, and even in the few remaining centers of orthodoxy the preacher confines himself to such a narrow compass that his people are scarcely any better indoctrinated at the end of the year than they were at the beginning: there is no longer a bringing forth of "things new" as well as "things old" (Matt. 13:52). How many of our readers, we wonder, ever heard a sermon on their duties and privileges in connection with sickness! Very, very few we fear. Little wonder that so many ill-informed members of "evangelical churches" fall such easy victims to modern religious fads.

It is no sufficient reply for preachers to say, We have far weightier and more essential themes to expound. True, the salvation of the soul is immeasurably greater than the healing of the body, nevertheless the Scriptures have much to say concerning the body, and it is to our very great loss if we ignore or remain ignorant about the same. Is it of no moment at all whether the Christian be healthy or sickly? Has our loving heavenly Father left His children without any instruction concerning the laws of health? And when they fall ill is their situation no better than that of the unbelieving world? Must they too lean upon the arm of flesh when sickness overtakes them, and seek the help of a doctor—often an infidel? The Lord is "a very present help in trouble" (Ps. 46:1): does that mean nothing more than that the saint must, in every instance, seek grace from Him to patiently endure his afflictions? God has promised to supply "all the need" of His people (Phil. 4:19): does that include nothing better than drugs and medicines, such as the Christ-rejecter has access to, when I am ill? These are not questions to be lightly dismissed, but prayerfully pondered in the light of Holy Writ.

If the Divine healing cults have gone to one extreme, that of unbalanced fanaticism, have not most of the Lord's people in this matter gone to the opposite extreme—that of unbelieving stoicism or fatalistic inertia? Is not the attitude of only too many something like this? O well, man is born unto trouble as the sparks fly upward, so as I cannot expect immunity from physical sufferings, hence I must take what remedies I can for relief, and then make the best of a bad job; or, since this be my appointed lot, I must endeavor to bear it as patiently as I can. Of course when pain is acute they cry unto the Lord and beg Him to ease their anguish, just as Pharaoh did when God's sore plagues were upon his land. And when Christians pray for recovery, how many of them really do so with the expectation of its being granted? how many know where to turn for a pertinent promise and then plead the same prevailingly? Yet some of them feel they are living beneath their privileges as sons and daughters of the Almighty, and when they hear or read what is advanced by the "faith healing" people wonder how much of it is true and how much false.

Arthur W. Pink

Chapter 2
The Subject of Health

Now it seems to us that we should begin with the subject of health, for prevention is better than cure. O what a priceless boon is a sound body and good health: a boon which is denied to some from birth, and which few really appreciate till it be taken from them. It has long impressed the writer what a remarkable thing it is that any of us enjoy any health at all, seeing that we have six thousand years of sinful heredity behind us! It is due alone to the goodness and kindness of God that the great majority enter this world with more or less sound bodies and reach youth in the bloom of health. But sin and folly then take heavy toll and the constitutions of millions are wrecked before middle life is reached. Nor is it always brought about by wicked intemperance and dissipation. Often it is the outcome of ignorance, through failure to heed some of the most elementary laws of hygiene. Alas the majority of people will learn in no other school than that of hard and bitter experience and consequently most of them only discover how to live when the time comes for them to die. True we cannot put old heads on young shoulders, yet if the inexperienced are too proud to heed the counsels of the mature then they must reap the consequences.

Now surely, other things being equal, the Christian ought to enjoy better health than the non-Christian. Why so? Why, because if his walk be regulated by God's Word he will at least be preserved from those diseases which are the fruit of certain transgressions. The English word "holiness" means wholeness, soundness. The more we are kept from sinning the more shall we escape its consequences. "Godliness is profitable unto all things (the body as well as the soul), having promise of the life that now is, and of that which is to come" (1 Tim. 4:8). One of the basic laws of health is the Sabbatic statute. "The Sabbath was made for man" (Mark 2:27), for his good, because he needed it. It was made for man that he might be a man, something more than a beast of burden or a human treadmill. His body needs it as truly as does his soul. This has been unmistakably demonstrated in this country. When France collapsed and the British Isles faced the most desperate crisis of their long history, the government foolishly ordered that those in the coal mines and munitions factories must work seven days a week, but they soon learned that the workmen produced less than they did in six days—they could not stand up to the additional strain.

By resting from manual toil on the Sabbath man is enabled to recuperate his strength for the labors of the week lying ahead, yet that cannot be accomplished by attending one meeting after another on that day, nor by exhausting one's strength through lengthy walks to and from the services—moving the tent nearer the altar is the remedy—still less by profaning the Sabbath in carnal "recreation." Another Divine precept which promotes health is, "he that believeth shall not make haste" (Isa. 28:16). Side by side with the speeding tempo of modern life we behold the multiplying nervous disorders, and those who are murdered or maimed on the highway. For many years we have avoided motor cars, buses and trains whenever the distance to be covered was not too great to walk, not using them more than two or three times in a twelve-month. Rushing around, hurrying and scurrying hither and thither, is not only injurious but a violation of the Divine rule: "He that hasteth with his feet sinneth" (Prov. 19:2)—which means exactly what it says.

"Take therefore no anxious thought for the morrow" (Matt. 6:34). How good health is promoted by obedience to this precept scarcely needs pointing out. It is carking care and worry which disturbs the mind, affects circulation, impairs digestion, and prevents restful sleep. If the Christian would cast all his care on the Lord (1 Pet. 5:7) what freedom from anxiety would be his. "The joy of the Lord is your strength" (Neh. 8:10)—physically as well as spiritually. What a tome to a wearied body and tired mind it is to delight ourselves in the Lord: "a merry heart doeth good like a medicine" (Prov. 17:22). "My son, attend to My words . . . for they are life unto those that find them and health to all his flesh" (Prov. 4:20, 22): do we really believe this? "Fear the Lord and depart from evil: it shall be health to thy navel and marrow to thy bones" (Prov. 3:7, 8).

Godly living is conducive to healthiness of mind and body, and other things being equal that will be one of its bi-products. By "other things being equal" we mean: as in the case of one who is not suffering for the sins of his father; who did not ruin his constitution by debauchery before conversion; and who exercises ordinary common sense in attending to the elementary rules of hygiene. One who is "temperate in all things" (1 Cor. 9:25) will escape many or all of those ills which is the price which has to be paid for intemperance. Scripture does not require us to be either Spartans or Epicureans but to "let our moderation be known unto all" (Phil. 4:5). God "giveth richly all things to enjoy" (1 Tim. 6:17), yet not to abuse. "Every creature of God is good and nothing to be refused" (1 Tim. 4:4) providing it is used aright, but His choicest creatures p rove harmful if used to excess. God has provided great variety in nature, and each one has to learn for himself what best suits him and deny himself of that which disagrees.

Chapter 3
The Duties and Privileges of Christians in Illness

What are the duties and privileges of the Christian when he falls ill? First, endeavor to ascertain the occasion and cause of his sickness. As intimated in the previous chapters, many physical ailments are due to inattention unto the most simple and obvious rules of hygiene. Much illness is brought about by our own carelessness and folly. Those guilty of gluttony are inviting trouble. But there are various forms of gluttony as well as degrees thereof. There is an intemperance of quality as well as of quantity. They who disdain plain and wholesome food, and who concentrate principally on fancy things and a rich diet must not be surprised if their systems become upset; in such cases a two or three days' complete fast, followed by a return to a simpler and saner mode of living, is the best remedy. Those with weak chests should not needlessly expose themselves to the night air. Wet shoes are to be removed as soon as possible if colds are to be avoided. If we ignore the dictates common prudence then we may easily discover what has injured and how to correct it.

But suppose upon careful reflection we are unable to trace our present ill health to any physical neglect or folly, then what are we to do? Seek to ascertain the moral cause thereof. "Let us search and try our ways" (Lam. 3:40), making an honest endeavor to find out what it is which has grieved the Spirit. If conscience be allowed to do her work the probability is we shall soon be made aware that there is an Achan in our camp, an Achan which must be dealt with unsparingly if we are to enjoy the smile of the Lord again. If we have set up some idol it must be thrown down; if we have indulged some lust it must be mortified: if we have entered a forbidden path it must be forsaken: if we have willfully departed from some path of duty it must be returned unto, otherwise "some worse thing" is likely to come upon us. All known sins must be judged, mourned over, confessed in detail unto God: "I said I will confess my transgressions unto the Lord, and Thou forgavest the iniquity of my sin" (Ps. 32:5).

But suppose after an honest and careful review of my ways conscience does not convict me of any particular sin, then what must I do? Prayerfully seek the help of the Holy Spirit. Get down before the Lord and cry "Search me, O God, and know my heart: try me and know my thoughts; and see if there be any wicked way in me, and lead me in the way everlasting" (Ps. 139:23, 24). Though there may be nothing in my outward conduct for which the Lord is chastising me, yet it is likely there is something within against which He is intimating His displeasure and for which He requires me to humble myself. A spirit of selfishness, the allowing of pride, the workings of self-will, the stirrings of rebellion when Divine Providence crosses me, the exercise of self-righteousness, may be the plague-spot of my soul which needs purging. In the rush and pressure of every-day life the "little foxes which spoil the vines" (Song of Sol. 2:15) are apt to be neglected, and if we are careless then we must not be surprised if we are placed on our backs for a season, that there may be time for reflection and opportunity for closer dealings between the soul and God, that the hidden things of darkness may be brought out into the light and faithfully dealt with.

Chapter 4
2 Chronicles 7:14 Considered

"If My people which are called by My name shall humble themselves, and pray, and seek My face, and turn from their wicked ways; then will I hear from heaven, and will forgive their sin, and will heal their land" (2 Chron. 7:14). This passage bears directly on our present subject and contains important and definite instruction for us. First, it shows that God sends physical judgments upon His people because of their transgressions. Second, it makes known what they are to do when the Divine rod falls upon them. Third, it contains a pertinent and precious promise for faith to lay hold of. Against this it may be objected that such a passage is not applicable to us; that God's dealings with His people in this Christian era are on very different principles than those which actuated Him under the Mosaic economy; that He dealt with them according to the Law, whereas He deals with us according to the riches of His grace. Such a contention is entirely unscriptural. God's governmental dealings are the same in all dispensations: maintaining the requirements of holiness and exercising mercy toward the penitent have ever characterized God's "ways." Had the O. T. regime been one of stern and unrelieved justice, there had been no "healing" promised upon repentance, for Law as such knows no pity and shows no mercy.

Let it be carefully noted that the teaching of the New Testament is precisely the same on this subject as in the Old Testament. "For he that eateth and drinketh unworthily eateth and drinketh damnation (judgment) to himself, not discerning the Lord's body. For this cause many are weak and sickly among you, and many sleep" (1 Cor. 11:29, 30). The Corinthians had been guilty of profaning the Lord's table, turning the holy Supper into a carnal feast. God would not tolerate such irreverence and impiety in this dispensation any more than He would under the Mosaic, and evidenced His sore displeasure by visiting them with a temporal judgment, smiting them in their bodies. Thus this passage is strictly analogous to that in 2 Chronicles 7. But more, as there so here, the remedy is also graciously made known: "For if we would judge ourselves we should not be judged" (v. 31). If the Corinthians would unsparingly condemn themselves for their unseemly conduct and mourn over it before God, His judgment would be removed and the many weak and sickly ones recovered and not be made to "sleep" (die). If we sit in judgment on ourselves we shall not be judged by the Lord. "But when we are judged, we are chastened of the Lord, that we should not be condemned with the world" (v. 31): God chastening us here that we may escape eternal woe hereafter.

Let us return then to 2 Chronicles 7:14. There we find the Lord's people being dealt with for their sins. A temporal judgment bears heavily upon them: how is deliverance therefrom to be obtained? First, they must "humble themselves." And what is meant by that? The same as in 1 Corinthians 11:31, "judge ourselves." A word in Leviticus 26:41 will supply the needed help: "if then their uncircumcised hearts be humbled and they then accept of the punishment of their iniquity, then will I remember My covenant." To "humble" ourselves beneath the rod of God is to cease asking, What have I done to deserve this? to stop resisting the rod, and meekly bowing thereto, acknowledging that my wicked conduct deserves it. David "humbled" himself when he owned "I know, O Lord, that Thy judgments are right, and that Thou in faithfulness hast afflicted me" (Ps. 119:75). To "judge ourselves" is to take sides with God against ourselves: not until we do so does the rod begin to obtain its designed effect. The "peaceable fruit of righteousness" is only obtained under Divine chastisement "unto them which are exercised thereby" (Heb. 12:11)—exercised in their conscience. We must "hear the rod" (Micah 6:9) if we are to profit therefrom, and when we have heard its rebuking message, endorse the righteousness of it.

"If My people which are called by My name shall humble themselves": that is the first thing, and it is vain to proceed further until it be properly attended to, for pride is more hateful to God than anything else. "And pray" is the next thing. Until we have truly humbled ourselves before God there can be no real prayer, but having taken our place in the dust and condemned ourselves, then we may make known our requests unto Him. And what is it, under such circumstances, that we most need to pray or? Surely for a deeper sense of His holiness and of our vileness, for a contrite and broken heart for faith in His mercy, for cleansing and restoration to fellowship. Such requests issue not from the Pharisee, but they are the breathings of humility. "And seek my face": is that but a repetition of the previous clause? No, it goes further: it expresses increased definiteness, diligence and fervor. The omniscient One cannot be imposed upon by mere lip service: He requires the heart. There has to be more than a bare asking, namely, a "seeking," and such a "seeking" that we actually "draw near" and have a face-to-face meeting with Him we have displeased. God will not gloss over our sins, neither must we.

"And turn from their wicked ways." It was their departure from the paths of righteousness and entering into forbidden territory which brought down upon them the displeasure and rod of the Holy One, and therefore if they are to be delivered from His judgment they must of necessity forsake their sins. "Turn from their wicked ways" with loathing and abhorrence, with no secret reserve but with firm purpose of heart to abandon them and go back to them no more (Ps. 85:8). Repentance is something more than sorrowing over the past: it includes the resolution there shall be no repetition in the future. Idols must be destroyed and not put away in a cupboard from which they may be taken out again. "Then will I hear from heaven, and will forgive their sin, and will heal their land." Here is the gracious promise. But mark well its opening "Then": only when its preceding conditions have been fully met: we have no warrant to look for its fulfillment until its qualifying terms are observed by us. Note too its scope: hearing from God is granted, forgiveness is assured, and healing is available for faith to claim.

"Then will I hear from heaven, and will forgive their sin, and will heal their land." (2 Chron. 7:14). We have no time to waste on any who would raise the quibble that this verse refers to the healing of "land" and not of our bodies. But some who perceive that the principles of this verse are pertinent to cases of personal affliction will ask, Are we then to understand that where God has visited His people with temporal judgment and they have complied with the conditions He has here specified, He will in every instance remove that judgment; that He will bestow immediate and complete healing? Ah! the terms of that question go beyond the terms of that promise: 2 Chronicles 7:14 neither says that He would heal their land "immediately" nor "completely." Nor must we when pondering the subject of Divine healing confine ourselves to this particular verse. For instance, we read that the men of Jericho sought unto Elisha on behalf of their ground, saying "the water is naught and the ground barren." And we are told the prophet said "Bring me a new cruse and put salt therein. And they brought it to him. And he went forth unto the springs of the waters and cast the salt in them and said, Thus saith the Lord, I have healed these waters; there shall not be from hence any more death or barren land" (2 Kings 2:21).

God could have healed those waters without any salt, as He could have made sweet the bitter waters at Marah without bidding Moses to cast a certain tree into them (Ex. 15:23-25). Sometimes the Lord is pleased to use means, and at other times to dispense with them: for He exercises His sovereignty here as elsewhere. Perhaps some will say, this makes the subject more complex and hence more perplexing. Doubtless, and God may have so designed it. The natural man wants everything to be made smooth and easy for him. But God's way is to stain human pride, to make us feel our insufficiency, to drive us to our knees. God would have our hearts to be exercised before Him, and instead of assuming we must now act in the same way as we did before in a similar situation, look to Him for instruction and directions. "My soul wait thou only upon God, for my expectation is from Him" (Ps. 62:5).

God is sovereign and does not act uniformly, and we are both responsible agents and utterly dependent upon Him, and therefore must act neither irrationally nor presumptuously. God is sovereign: He did not always afflict Israel's land with drought or pestilence when they displeased Him, nor does He afflict the Christian's body each time he backslides or forsakes the highway of holiness. And when God did cause His judgment to fall upon Israel's land, He did not always remove His stroke as soon as confession of sin was made and reformation of conduct was affected; nor will He in every instance removed sickness when the afflicted one acknowledges his fault and does his "first works." And, as already pointed out, when God was pleased to heal Israel's land sometimes it was by blessing the means of His own appointing, and at other times it was without the use of any means at all. Thus it is when He heals our bodies. To one blind man Christ gave sight instantly, but to another He put His hands on his eyes a second time before he was fully restored (Mark 8:22-25).

Divine Healing: Is It Scriptural?

Does someone say, All of this seems very confusing and gets me nowhere. No doubt it is so to the carnal mind. It is for the tried child of God we write and not for those who wish to be spared all exercise of heart, like patients going to a doctor for a prescription so that nothing is required of them but to hand it to the chemist for him to make up. As intimated at the beginning of the preceding paper, the first duty of the ailing Christian is to inquire into the occasion or cause of his sickness: whether it be due to imprudence or intemperance, whether God be chastening him for some breach of His Law, or whether there be some other reason for it, for afflictions are sometimes sent upon the saints for their refining and pruning rather than for correction, that they may yield some of the choicest of all the spiritual fruits. Thus the believer who desires light on his situation must wait upon the Lord and say "show me wherefore Thou contendest with me" (Job 10:2).

If the Lord has shown that the sickness is a mark of His displeasure because we have followed some wicked way, then our course is clear, namely, to conduct ourselves according to the requirements of 2 Chronicles 7:14. Having done so, then what? Appropriate its promise, yet meekly and not presumptuously. Having righted the wrong before God, having obtained His ear, now plead His Word. Say, Lord, I have sought to humble myself, pray, and seek Thy face, and renounce my wicked ways, and Thou assurest me Thou wilt forgive and heal me: do as Thou hast said. But Lord, I am a poor ignorant creature and knowest not Thy mind: what wouldest Thou have me to do? Is it Thy pleasure to lay Thy restoring hand upon me this very moment? If so, enable me to trust in Thee with all my heart; or wouldest Thou have me to use some means? if so, graciously direct my mind and hand to them and cause me to count upon Thy making them efficacious unto me, so that I may trust Thee and not them, that the glory may be all Thine own.

Arthur W. Pink

Chapter 5
The Pertinence of Matthew 9:29

"According to your faith be it unto you" (Matt. 9:29) is most pertinent unto our present inquiry. God is pledged to honor faith wherever He finds it: never does He fail those who trust Him fully; no, not when they count upon Him working a miracle, as many can testify. But what is the "faith" here spoken of? It is one which rests upon the sure Word of God. It is one which is made up of two chief elements: expectation and submission. There are some who suppose those two things are subversive of each other, that the attitude of not my will but Thine be done makes real expectation impossible. But that is wrong, through a mistaken conception of what spiritual expectation consists of. Let it first be said that where there is not first genuine resignation there can be no true expectation. Spiritual submission is spreading my case before the Lord and asking Him to deal with it as He sees best, and if I count upon His wisdom and goodness, that is the exercise of faith; and if I have confidence that He will do so, that is the expectation of faith—the expectation not that He will grant what my carnal nature desires, but that He will give what is most for His glory and my highest good; anything other than that is not faith but presumption.

Some bodily infirmities are produced by the devil, probably more than are commonly suspected. Job's boils were caused by him, and we read of a daughter of Abraham "whom Satan hath bound, lo, these eighteen years" (Luke 13:16). Certainly it is neither an honor to the Lord nor a credit to His child for one of them to be overcome by the Enemy. Nor need he be, for it is written "Resist the devil, and he will flee from you" (James 4:7), to which should be added "whom resist steadfastly in the faith" (1 Pet. 5:9). Many years ago it was arranged that we should speak in a certain city church, and a few hours before the service we were suddenly attacked by a heavy cold and developed a high temperature. The friends with whom we were staying urged us to cancel the engagement and phone another preacher to deputize, for it was pouring with rain and a long walk was before us. But we realized that Satan was hindering and committed ourselves into the hands of our Master, counting upon Him to protect us from any harm. He did so, and the next morning we were quite normal. On another occasion we lost our voice and could speak in only a hoarse whisper, but we trusted the Lord to undertake, and preached for an hour and a half without any inconvenience and could easily be heard in the remotest corners of the large building; yet as soon as we left the pulpit we could not speak at all. No, He never fails those who trust HIM.

The subject is many-sided and much has to be left unsaid. It is clear to us that many Christians are living below their privileges in this matter. "Jehovah-Rophi" ("The Lord that healeth thee": Ex. 15:26) is as truly one of His titles as "Jehovah-Tsidkneu"("The Lord our righteousness": Jer. 23:5), yet how few count upon Him as such, having more confidence in human physicians and their medicines. Fewer still seem to know anything about trusting the Lord for the body (1 Cor. 6:13). It is written "the prayer of faith shall save the sick" (James 5:15), yet the exercise of faith is not subject to a mere effort of the will. It is our duty to pray "Lord, increase our faith," yet that prayer will not be answered unless we use what we already have (Luke 8:18). Broadly speaking, when sickness prevents the discharge of duty, it is our privilege to count upon the Lord to remove the hindrance.

Here let it be said, we are far from affirming that all who resort to material remedies are missing the Lord's best, though in many instances that is probably the case; nor that God is always ready to heal if we trust Him. Rather is it His will that some should glorify Him "in the fires" (Isa. 24:15). God sent an angel to deliver Peter from prison, but suffered Stephen to be stoned to death. Some plants thrive best in burning heat, whereas ferns flourish in the shade. Certain graces, like zeal and intrepidity, are exercised on the battlefield, whereas meekness and patience are developed under suffering. God does not intend that many should do such a work as Geo. Muller did and therefore He gives not faith for it, and those who imitate him fail. The privilege and duty of each Christian is defined in "Commit thy way unto the Lord: trust also in Him, and He shall bring to pass" (Isa. 37:5). Bring what to pass? His way, the best way, though it may be the very opposite of what you wish. Commit thy case unto Him, trustfully, and leave Him to decide what will be most for His glory. If sickness persists, beg God to sanctify it to you.

Chapter 6
Appendix on James 5:14-16

A number of friends who appreciated our recent articles on this subject have written to us expressing the desire for a few words on James 5:14-16. We respond to their wish with a certain amount of diffidence, for we are not sure in our own mind either as to its interpretation or application. This is a passage which has long been an occasion of controversy and debate, and those who took part therein found—as is often the case—that it was easier to refute the arguments of their opponents than to establish their own position. When we are uncertain about the meaning of Scripture we usually remain silent thereon, but in this instance we will give the leading views which have been expressed, and state how we feel toward them.

First, Romanists insist that this "anointing with oil" is a standing ordinance in the church and James 5:14, 15 is the principal passage appealed to by them in support of their dogma and practice of "extreme unction." But here as everywhere the papists go contrary to the Scriptures, for instead of anointing the sick as a healing ordinance, they only administer it to those at the point of death. We have no hesitation in denouncing their perversion as a mere hypocritical pageantry. The "unction" they use must be olive oil mixed with balsam, consecrated by a bishop, who must nine times bow the knee, saying thrice "Ave sanctum oleum" (Hail, holy oil), and thrice "Ave Sanctum chrisma" (Hail, holy chrism), and thrice more, "Ave, sanctum Balsamum" (Hail, holy balsam). The members anointed are the eyes, ears, nose, mouth, and for the extremities, the reins and feet: in women, the navel. The design thereof is, the expulsion of the relics of sin and to equip the soul for its conflicts with the powers of evil in the moment of death. One has but to mention these things to reveal their absurdity.

Second, the position generally taken by the Reformers and Puritans, was, that this anointing the sick with oil was not designed as a sacrament, they being but two in number: baptism and the

Lord's supper. They pointed out that so far from this being a standing rite, the apostles themselves seldom used oil in the healing of the sick: they wrought cures by a touch (Acts 3:7), by their shadow (Acts 5:15), by handkerchiefs (Acts 19:12), by laying on of hands (Acts 28:8), by word of mouth (Acts 9:34). Nor does it appear that they were permitted to employ this gift indiscriminately, no not even among brethren in Christ dear to them, or why should Paul leave Trophimus at Miletum sick (2 Tim. 4:20) or sorrow so much over the illness of Epaphroditus (Phil. 2:27)? In this too God exercised His sovereignty. But what is more to the point, this supernatural endowment was only of brief duration: "But that grace of healing has disappeared, like all other miraculous powers, which the Lord was pleased to exhibit for a time, that He might render the power of the Gospel, which was then new, the object of admiration forever" (Calvin).

A list of the "charismata" or supernatural gifts which obtained during the apostolic period is found in 1 Corinthians 12: "to another faith, by the same Spirit; to another the gift of healing, by the same Spirit; to another the working of miracles, to another prophecy, to another discerning of spirits, to another divers kinds of tongues, to another the interpretation of tongues" (vv. 9, 10.). They were designed chiefly for the authenticating of Christianity and to confirm it in heathen countries. Their purpose, then, was only a temporary one, and as soon as the canon of Scripture was closed they were withdrawn. As 1 Corinthians 13 plainly intimates "whether there be prophecies (inspired messages from God) they shall fail (to be given any more); whether there be tongues, they shall cease; whether there be (supernatural) knowledge, it shall vanish away" (v. 8). It was the view of Matthew Henry, Thomas Manton, John Owen, and in fact nearly all of the Puritan divines, that James 5:14, 15 refers to the exercise of one of those supernatural gifts which the church enjoyed only in the first century.

Among the leading arguments advanced in support of this contention are the following. First, the "anointing with oil" clearly appears to look back to Mark 6:13 where we are told of the twelve, they "anointed with oil many that were sick, and healed them." Second, the positive promise of healing, verse 15, seems to be an unconditional and general one, as though no exceptions, no cases of failure, were to be looked for. Third, "healing" was certainly one of the miraculous gifts specified in 1 Corinthians 12. Moreover,

Divine Healing: Is It Scriptural?

it hardly seems likely that the "faith" here mentioned is an ordinary one: though whether it differed in kind or only in degree is not easy to determine. There was the "faith of miracles"—either to work them or the expectation of them on the part of those who were the beneficiaries, as is clear from Matthew 21:24; Mark 11:24; 1 Corinthians 13:2. The "anointing with oil" after the praying over the sick is regarded as a seal or pledge of the certainty of healing or recovery.

On the other side, we find such a deeply-taught man and so able an expositor as Thomas Goodwin (1600-1680) insisting on the contrary. He pointed out, first, that James 5:14 is quite different from Mark 6:13, for here the anointing with oil is joined with prayer, whereas prayer is not mentioned there, but only the miraculous gift. Second, the ones to be sent for were not specified as men endowed with the gift of healing, but the "elders," and there is nothing to show that all of them possessed that gift. The "elders" were standing officers who were to continue. Third, the ones to be healed are the "sick" or infirm, but extraordinary healing would have extended further—to the blind, the deaf and dumb, and would have reached to unbelievers instead of being restricted to church members: cf. 1 Corinthians 14:22. Fourth, the means commanded: oil and prayer on all such occasions, whereas the extraordinary gift of healing was not so confined, but was frequently effected without any means at all, by mere word of mouth.

Third, rather more than a century ago, a certain Edward Irving, founder of the "Catholic Apostolic Church," propounded the theory that the supernatural gifts which existed in the early Church had been lost through the unbelief and carnality of its members, and that if there was a return to primitive order and purity, they would again be available. Accordingly he appointed "apostles," and "prophets" and "evangelists." They claimed to speak in tongues, prophesy, interpret and work miracles. There is little doubt in our mind that this movement was inspired by Satan, and probably a certain amount of abnormal phenomena attended it, though much of it was explainable as issuing from a state of high nervous tension and hysteria. Irving's theory, with some modifications and some additions has been popularized and promulgated by the more recent so-called 'Pentecostal movement," where a species of unintelligible jabbering and auto-suggestion cum mesmerism is styled "speaking in tongues," and "faith healing." Many of their devotees and dupes attempt to carry out James 5:14, 15, but with very meager and unsatisfactory results.

Fourth, there is the grotesque idea of the Dispensationalists. These is a class of men who pose as being exceptionally enlightened, and under the guise of "rightly dividing the Word of Truth" arbitrarily partition the Scriptures, affirming "this is not for us," "that does not pertain to this present era of Grace," "that relates to the Tribulation period," "this will be fulfilled in the Millennium." Because the opening verse of James reads, "To the twelve tribes which are scattered abroad, greetings," these robbers of God's children declare this epistle is "entirely Jewish;" as well might they reason that the first epistle of Paul is designed only for Papists because it is addressed "To all that be in Rome" (Rom. 1:1). The epistle of James belongs to all the "beloved brethren," to all born-again souls (1:16, 18). It is surely striking that the very passage we are here considering (5:14-16) comes right between a reference to Job (a Gentile) who endured patiently his affliction and found the Lord to be "pitiful and of tender mercy" (v. 11) and to Elijah who is described as "a man subject to like passions as we are" yet mighty in prayer (v. 17)—as though the Spirit was anticipating and refuting this mad notion.

Now where such widely-different interpretations are given of a passage, it usually follows that the true one lies somewhere between two extremes, and such we believe is the case here. We are very loathe to regard our passage as being an obsolete one, that it refers to something which pertained only to the apostolic age and relates not at all to us. When referring to the Papish travesty of this "anointing with oil" Thomas Goodwin said, "The Reformed churches seeing that such a sacrament could not be and this must needs be a perversion of it, did justly reject it, only in rejecting it (as in some other things) they went too far, even denying it to have that use of restoring the sick as a seal of the promise, and an indefinite means to convey that blessing which God in mercy hath appointed it to be." We are strongly inclined to agree with this eminent Puritan that the churches which grew out of the Reformation went too far when they set aside this passage as containing Divine directions to be followed by Gospel churches throughout this Christian era. Such a sweeping conclusion needs qualifying.

The knotty point to be settled is, how far and at which points is this qualification to be made? Personally we believe the general principle and promise of the passage holds good for all generations—seasons of great spiritual declension and deadness only excepted. In normal times it is the privilege of the saint—when seriously ill, or suffering great pain, and not on every light occasion—to send for the "elders" (pastors, ministers) of the local Gospel church to which he belongs, for they who preach God's Word to him should surely be the fittest to spread his case before Him: cf. Job 42:8. They are to pray over him, commending him to the mercy of God and seeking recovery for him if that be according to the Divine will: whether or not the "anointing with oil" should accompany the praying is a detail on which we are not prepared to dogmatize; but where the sick one desires it, his request should be complied with. The kind of oil is not specified, though most likely olive oil was used in the first century.

It should be pointed out that those promises of God which relate to temporal and eternal mercies are quite different from those pertaining to spiritual and eternal things, the former being general and indefinite and not unconditional and absolute as are many of the latter, and therefore as God reserves to Himself the freedom to make them good when, as, and to whom He pleases, we must ask in full submission to His sovereign pleasure. To illustrate: if I am starting out on a journey I ask God to preserve me from all harm and danger if that be His holy will (Rom. 1:10), but I make no such proviso when I request Him to deliver me from those who assault my soul (2 Tim. 4:18). Thus "the prayer of faith" here is not a definite expectation that God will heal, but a peaceful assurance that He will do that which is most for His glory and the sick one good. That the promise of James 5:15 is an indefinite and not an absolute one is clear from this consideration: if it were not so, he could continually claim the promise and so never die— the "and IF he have committed sins" further confirms the indefiniteness of what is here in view.

Some are likely to object against what has been pointed out in the last paragraph and say, But faith must have a foundation to rest upon, and it has none other than the Word of God: if then there be here no definite promise to lay hold of and plead before God, the "prayer of faith" is impossible, for there is no assurance the sick one will be healed. That may sound very plausible and pious, yet it is wrong. There is a faith of reliance and submission as well as a faith of expectation. There is no higher, no stronger, no grander faith than one which has such confidence in the wisdom and goodness of God as leads me to present my case to Him and say "Do as seemeth Thee good." It is always a help when we can plead a promise, but God is greater than all His promises and where some specific need or emergency be not covered by some express promise, faith may count upon the mercy and power of God Himself— this is what Abraham did: Hebrews 11:19!

Personally we greatly fear that there are very few "elders" now left on earth whom it would be any good to send for in an emergency: only those living close to God and blessed with strong faith would be of any use. This is a day of "small things," nevertheless the Lord remains unchanged and ready to show Himself strong on behalf of those who walk uprightly. Though there be no spiritual elders available, yet God is accessible; seek unto Him, and if He grants you the "prayer of faith" then healing is certain either by natural means or by supernatural intervention. "The Lord is undoubtedly present with His people to assist them in all ages, and when necessary He heals their diseases as much as He did in ancient times; but He does not display those miraculous powers or dispense miracles by the hands of apostles, because that gift was only of temporary duration" (Calvin)

"Confess your faults one to another, and pray one for another, that ye may be healed" (v. 16). Here the scope of our passage is widened: in verse 13 the afflicted or tried one is to pray for himself, in verse 14 the ministers are to pray for the one seriously sick, now fellow-Christians are to pray for each other. But first they are bidden to confess their faults one to another, which does not mean revealing the secrets of their hearts or acquainting their brethren with that which is suited only for the ear of God: but cases where they have tempted or injured one another or consented to the same evil act—tattling, for example. A mutual acknowledgement of those faults which cause coldness and estrangement, exciting one another to repentance for the same, promotes the spirit of prayer and fellowship, The "healing" here is also wider, referring primarily to that of the soul (Ps. 41:4) and breaches (Heb. 12:13), being the term used in 1 Peter 2:24, yet also includes removal of physical chastisements.

Observations in Conclusion

A few brief observations on our passage in conclusion.

Personal prayer (v. 13) is enjoined before ministerial (v. 14) and social (v. 16): individual responsibility cannot be shelved.

God is not indifferent to the sickness of His people (v. 14), but cares for their bodies as well as their souls.

Are not ministers too free in visiting the sick and praying over them, instead of waiting until they are sent for (v. 14)?

If none but "elders" (ministers) were to anoint with oil, surely they alone are eligible to administer baptism and the Lord's supper!

All sickness is not occasioned by sin or the "if" of verse 15 would be meaningless.

Yet God does sometimes visit with physical chastisements as the "if" denotes.

The mutual confession of verse 16 refutes the Papish error of "auricular confession," for the priest does not confess his sins to those revealing to him the secrets of their souls!

Printed in February 2023
by Rotomail Italia S.p.A., Vignate (MI) - Italy